LOVE FOR EVER MERIDIAN

Published jointly in the US and UK

Cross-Cultural Communications
Stanley H. Barkan, Editor-Publisher
239 Wynsum Avenue
Merrick, NY 11566 USA
cccpoetry@aol.com
www.cross-culturalcommunications.com

The Seventh Quarry Press
Peter Thabit Jones, Editor-Publisher
Dan-y-bryn, 74 Cwm Level Road
Brynhyfryd, Swansea SA5 9DY Wales
info@peterthabitjones.com
www.peterthabitjones.com

Library of Congress Control Number: 2011040464

ISBN 978-0-89304-379-7
978-0-89304-380-3 (pbk)

Front cover photograph of Swansea Bay and back cover photograph of
River Tâf, Laugharne, by Peter Thabit Jones.

Frontispiece photograph by Lisa Maroski. Bust of Dylan Thomas by
Hugh Oloff De Wet, Charles Deering McCormick Library of Special
Collections, Northwestern University Library.

Printed in USA

CONTENTS

Prologue

An Unexpected Adventure

In November 2008, I traveled to Wales at the invitation of Welsh poet Peter Thabit Jones. Peter lives in Swansea, the birthplace of Dylan Thomas, and is founder and editor of *The Seventh Quarry*, a quarterly journal of international poetry. I had met Peter and Aeronwy Thomas, daughter of Dylan Thomas, in May 2008 in Monterey, California, where I live, on their Dylan Thomas Memorial Tour of America. The tour was organized by Stanley H. Barkan, poet, publisher of Cross-Cultural Communications, in consultation with Vince Clemente, both of New York. Working with Elliot Ruchowitz-Roberts of the Robinson Jeffers Tor House Foundation in Carmel and members of the Monterey Peninsula Friends of C. G. Jung, I had hosted Aeronwy and Peter for their West Coast events.

Peter has established *The Seventh Quarry Presents*, a series of readings including US poets in Wales, coordinated with Stan. Plans developed for Robin Metz of Chicago and me to read in Swansea and in the village of Laugharne, where Dylan and his wife Caitlin resided at various times, including the final years of his life.

In due course, then, I joined Robin and his wife, dramatist-scholar Elizabeth Carlin-Metz, in Swansea, with

Peter as guide. Aeronwy joined our pilgrimage to Fern Hill in Carmarthenshire and to the Boat House in Laugharne, her childhood home, where she performed her poems along with Robin and me.

My memoir of this experience, first written as a series of email messages, begins after the following chronology.

CONTEXT

Dylan Thomas in the 20th Century

Human kind cannot bear much reality.
—T. S. Eliot

As a context, I have compiled the following, eclectic chronology of the 20th century, particularly the first half, keying largely on the life and work of Dylan Thomas—the biographical facts and the themes.

Barbara W. Tuchman, in *The Proud Tower: A Portrait of the World Before the War, 1890–1914*, describes that period as "above all the culmination of a century of the most accelerated change in man's record . . . . The industrial and scientific revolutions had transformed the world. Man had entered the Nineteenth Century using only his own and animal power, supplemented by that of wind and water, much as he had entered the Thirteenth, or, for that matter, the First. He entered the Twentieth with his capacities in transportation, communication, production, manufacture and weaponry multiplied a thousandfold . . . ."

1900   World population is 1.65 billion. Nietzsche
        dies, and Freud introduces psychoanalysis and
        the theory of the unconscious in *The Interpreta-
        tion of Dreams*. Max Planck establishes the basis
        of quantum theory. In Britain, life expectancy
        is forty-five years for newborn boys, forty-nine
        years for girls.

1901   Victoria, Queen of the United Kingdom of
        Great Britain and Ireland, Empress of India,
        dies, ending her reign of sixty-three years. The
        crown passes to Edward VII. In the industrial
        port of Swansea, South Wales, having taken a
        new position on the faculty at Swansea
        Grammar School, D. J. Thomas, age twenty-
        five, meets seamstress Florence Williams, age
        nineteen.

1903   The Wright Brothers achieve the first sus-
        tained, controlled, powered flight. *The Great
        Train Robbery* is the first moving picture to tell
        a complete story. With completion of the
        Pacific Cable between San Francisco and
        Hawaii, a message from Teddy Roosevelt is
        conveyed around the globe in twelve minutes.
        Marconi transmits a radio greeting from TR to
        Edward VII. In Swansea, D. J. Thomas and
        Florrie Williams are married.

1904   In England, Ernest Rutherford and Frederick
        Soddy publish *The General Theory of Radio-
        activity*, based on J. J. Thomson's discovery of
        the electron, which was the basis for develop-
        ment of radio broadcasting.

1905   Freud publishes *Three Treatises on the Theory of*

Sex. Working in a Swiss patent office, Einstein publishes four papers, eventually called the *Annus Mirabilis* (Miraculous Year) *Papers*, that revolutionize physics and lead to the development of nuclear weapons. A building on West 23rd Street, erected in 1884 as the tallest building in New York, is established as the Hotel Chelsea.

1906   Voice and music are broadcast for the first time. In their rented home near Swansea Grammar School, Florrie and D. J. have their first child, a daughter, Nancy.

1909   Wilhelm Johannsen coins the term "gene."

1911   Rutherford establishes a model of the atom with a nucleus surrounded by orbiting electrons. The dropping of a bomb from an aircraft is first tested.

1912   The RMS *Titanic* sinks on its maiden voyage.

1913   In New York, painter Marcel Duchamp's *Nude Descending a Staircase* scandalizes the Armory Show. In Paris, Stravinsky's portrayal of fertility rites in *The Rite of Spring* leads to catcalls, whistles, fistfights, and a riot requiring police intervention at intermission. Rising to peak production, the 620 coal mines of South Wales employ over 250,000 men. In London, in December, of Irish parents, Caitlin Macnamara is born.

1914   In August, Austria declares war on Serbia, Germany declares war on Russia and France,

Germany invades Belgium, Britain and Serbia declare war on Germany, Austria declares war on Russia, Britain and France declare war on Austria—the Great War begins. In a new housing development in the Uplands, the prosperous west side of Swansea, D. J. and Florrie Thomas purchase a new home, No. 5 Cwmdonkin Drive. With construction not completed, **Dylan Marlais Thomas is born on October 27.** The middle name is that of his great uncle, William Thomas, a respected clergyman and accomplished poet who took the bardic name Gwilym Marles. Though both parents speak it fluently, the Welsh language is taught to neither of their children.

1916   On July 1, the first day of the Battle of the Somme, 58,000 British troops fall, one third of them killed. The attack is launched on a thirty-kilometer front north of the River Somme. The offensive ends on November 18 after British and French forces gain twelve kilometers of ground at the cost of 420,000 British and 200,000 French casualties. German casualties are estimated at 500,000.

1917   Lenin leads the Marxist revolution in Russia.

1918   The Great War ends with fifteen million dead. Great Britain has 900,000 dead, two million wounded. Ernest Rutherford splits an atom. Spengler publishes *The Decline of the West*.

1919   Twenty-two million die in a worldwide outbreak of influenza, greatest pandemic since the Black Death.

1922   T. S. Eliot publishes *The Waste Land*.

1923   In the first live trans-Atlantic radio broadcast,
        WJZ, New York, airs dance music from the
        Savoy Hotel in London. William Butler Yeats
        wins the Nobel Prize.

1924   Two Douglas World Cruiser airplanes circum-
        navigate the Earth from Seattle to Seattle. D. H.
        Lawrence publishes *Lady Chatterley's Lover*.

1925   At the Mount Wilson observatory in Pasadena,
        California, Edwin Hubble confirms the
        existence of galaxies beyond the Milky Way. In
        Germany, Hitler publishes *Mein Kampf*.
        Meeting in an upstairs hotel room during the
        National Eisteddfod—a Welsh festival of
        literature, music, and performance—six men
        form Plaid Cymru, the Party of Wales. Ten-
        year-old Dylan Thomas concludes his studies
        at Mrs. Hole's Dame School on Mirador
        Crescent, a few streets away from Cwmdonkin
        Drive. He then enters Swansea Grammar
        School where his father has risen to Senior
        English Master. Dylan's first poem is
        published in the school magazine. Richard
        Burton, who will become among the world's
        most famous film actors, is born as Richard
        Jenkens in Port Talbot, east of Swansea.

1926   The world's first scheduled airline service
        begins. In Britain, the Electricity Supply Act
        sets a goal of interconnecting power stations
        into a national grid, a project largely realized
        by 1935.

1927   Lindbergh flies *The Spirit of Saint Louis* from
            New York to Paris. The BBC is established
            under a Royal Charter.

1928   Thomas Hardy dies. Niels Bohr announces the
            principle of complementarity, establishing that
            phenomena such as light and electrons have
            both wavelike and particle-like characteristics.
            Mickey Mouse appears in *Steamboat Willie*, the
            first animated cartoon with a soundtrack.

1929   Hubble observes the universal recession of
            galaxies, which leads to development of the
            Big Bang Theory. In the Soviet Union, collec-
            tivization of agriculture brings about the
            deaths of millions of peasants by murder and
            starvation. The Swansea and Mumbles Rail-
            way is electrified. Established in 1807, the
            railway offered the world's first passenger
            railway service (on the same day that the
            British Parliament outlawed the transporting
            of Africans into slavery). Carriages were first
            pulled by horses. Later, trains were powered
            by sail, steam, battery, petrol, diesel, and
            finally electricity.

1930   Human population nears two billion. The first
            human egg cell is observed. Freud publishes
            Civilization and Its Discontents. The last oyster-
            harvesting skiff is retired in Mumbles, also
            known as Oystermouth. The oyster beds of
            Swansea Bay—considered the most prolific in
            Britain—were likely harvested by large groups
            of Roman slaves. Strong trade continued
            through the Middle Ages. Most beds were

eliminated in the early 1920s because of over-fishing and disease.

1931 At 102 stories, the Empire Sate Building in New York is the world's tallest building (until 1971). Caitlin Macnamara and Vivien John (daughter of the aged Augustus John, a flamboyant and highly regarded painter) travel to London where Caitlin, a freestyle dancer, begins a two-year dancing course. Dylan, age sixteen, leaves Swansea Grammar School and takes a job, arranged for him, as a junior reporter on *The South Wales Daily Post*.

1932 British physicists John Douglas Cockcroft and Ernest Thomas Sinton Walton achieve the first artificial nuclear disintegration. Aldous Huxley publishes *Brave New World*. Dylan leaves the *Daily Post* but continues to write freelance. He joins the Swansea Little Theatre Company, based in Mumbles, and with his sister Nancy performs in Noel Coward's *Hay Fever*. Dylan drinks companionably at the Antelope Hotel and The Mermaid in Mumbles. He frequents the cinema, with passions ranging from Hollywood classics to films of Luis Buñuel.

1933 Florrie Thomas's sister Annie dies. Dylan's childhood included regular summer trips to Fern Hill, his Aunt Annie's dairy farm in Dylan's ancestral Carmarthenshire, in the area of Laugharne, a medieval village. With Vera Gribben, Caitlin travels to Paris and stays a year. In May, Dylan's poem "And death shall have no dominion" is published in London; his first publication outside Wales. In August, nineteen-year-old Dylan travels to London for the first time, staying with sister Nancy and her husband. Dylan introduces himself to editors of London literary magazines.

1934   Commissioned by Hitler, Leni Riefenstahl directs *Triumph des Willens* (Triumph of the Will), filmed at the Nazi Party Convention at Nuremberg, introducing Nazi leaders to Germany and to the world. In *Bright Eyes*, Shirley Temple sings "On The Good Ship Lollipop." *Tropic of Cancer*, by Henry Miller, is published. After additional trips to London, Dylan moves there, returning frequently to his parents' house on Cwmdonkin Drive. As a prize for winning a poetry competition in London, Dylan's first book, *18 Poems*, is published, a month after his twentieth birthday. He has already written most of the poems for which he will become famous, collecting them in his Notebooks.

1936   Charles Chaplin releases *Modern Times*. Edward VIII abdicates. In Wales, three members of Plaid Cymru set fire to a Royal Air Force bombing school to protest the training center and destruction of an historic house in Penyberth; their action and subsequent imprisonment escalate attention to their cause. With slackening demand for coal, the effects of the global depression are acutely felt in the valleys of Wales. Dylan harvests his Notebooks for another collection published as *Twenty-Five Poems*. A second edition of *18*

Poems is printed. Dylan has lunch with T. S. Eliot. In April, at the Wheatsheaf public house in the West End, Augustus John introduces Dylan to Caitlin—who is John's lover at the time. Dylan and Caitlin allegedly stay together at the Eiffel Tower Hotel for a few days, charging their stay to John's account. Dylan attends the International Surrealist Exhibition, with Salvador Dali participating, in June. The next month, Dylan and Caitlin meet again in Laugharne at Castle House, home of novelist Richard Hughes.

1937   In China, Mao Zedong and the Red Army complete the 6,000-mile Long March. In Britain, Alan Turing, Alonso Church, and Emil Post work out the principles of modern computers. In April, in the London studios of the BBC, Dylan records his first radio broadcast, "Life and the Modern Poet." Defying his parents, Dylan and Caitlin marry in July. Caitlin meets the Thomases for the first time in Gower, where they now reside. Later, Dylan and Caitlin stay in Hampshire with her mother.

1938   In Germany, the Holocaust begins with *Kristallnacht* as twenty to thirty thousand Jews are carried off to concentration camps. Within seven years, six million Jews and eight million other "racial inferiors"—including Poles, Slavs, and Roma (Gypsies)—are put to death. Dylan and Caitlin move to Laugharne, occupying a small fisherman's cottage named "Eros." Later they move to a residence named "Sea View" for the "happiest period of our lives together," as later described by Caitlin. In August, Dylan publishes a collection of poems and stories titled *The Map of Love*. In October, he participates with W. H. Auden, Louis MacNeice, Kathleen Raine, and Stephen Spender in a BBC broadcast "The Modern Muse."

1939   In January, Caitlin gives birth to Llewelyn, their first child and first son. Opening the New York World's Fair, Franklin D. Roosevelt is the first world leader to deliver a televised speech. On September 3, Hitler sends his army into Poland, and Great Britain declares war on Germany. HCE, Here-Comes-Everybody, is the hero of *Finnegan's Wake* by James Joyce. *The Wonderful Wizard of Oz* is released. Dylan's first publication in America is a selection of poems and stories, *The World I Breathe*.

1940   In April, *Portrait of the Artist as a Young Dog*, a collection of Dylan's stories, is published in Britain and then in the US. Charlie Chaplin releases *The Great Dictator*, reportedly viewed twice by Hitler. Hitler watches films avidly; intelligence reports say that Hitler obtained the *Sieg Heil* salute from watching films of cheerleaders at American football games. In May, Dylan—who wants to avoid military service—fails his medical exam and is designated C3, lowest preference. Dylan and Caitlin leave Laugharne for London. In September, Dylan is engaged by Strand Films, with work that continues through the war, and the Nazi Blitz begins. Between mid-September and mid-November, 100 to 200 bombers attack London every night but one. Edward R. Murrow reports on radio to the US, the first live broadcasts from a theatre of war. In October, John Lennon is born in Liverpool, also a target of Nazi bombing. By mid-November, the Germans have dropped more than 13,000 tons of high explosive and more than one million incendiary bombs. On the evening of December 29, the German attack on the City of London causes what has been called the Second Great Fire of London.

1941   In February, Hitler orders the Luftwaffe to concentrate on British ports, and fifty-one attacks are made through May. Swansea is attacked on February 21 in the "three nights' blitz." The Swansea and Mumbles Railway survives the bombing, and its bright red trams become symbols of survival. After a visit to Swansea, Thomas writes a radio play, "Return Journey," that will be broadcast in 1947. In Duluth, Minnesota, Robert Allen Zimmerman (Bob Dylan) is born on May 24. By the end of May, over 43,000 British civilians, half in London, have been killed by Nazi bombing. More than a million houses in London have been destroyed or damaged.

1942   Overcoming the Japanese in the Battle of Midway in June, American military-industrial power ascends. In Chicago, Fermi directs the first controlled, self-sustaining nuclear chain reaction. At Peenemünde in Germany, the Space Age begins with the launch of a V-2 manufactured in underground caverns where Jewish slave laborers work on assembly lines; of sixty thousand workers, more than one-third do not survive the war. Dylan and Caitlin rent a flat at Wentworth Studios. Paul McCartney is born in June.

1943   US industry produces a ship a day and an airplane every five minutes. Alan Turing builds Colossus, among the first programmable electronic computers, used to decipher German communications. Dylan works continuously, ultimately participating in over 200 broadcasts. In February, *New Poems* is published in the US. In March, Aeronwy is born in London.

1944   George Orwell publishes *Animal Farm*. Germany attacks London and the south east with V-1 flying bombs and V-2 rockets. Dylan and Caitlin leave London to avoid the air raids, for a while staying with Donald Taylor, who employs Dylan as a BBC scriptwriter. As he and Caitlin move from place to place, Dylan writes poems and continues to develop *Under Milk Wood*, a "play for voices" that he has long had in mind. D-Day is June 6.

1945   In New Mexico, on July 16, 5:29:45 a.m., Mountain War Time, the first atomic bomb is detonated. Robert Oppenheimer names the event "Trinity." Some Manhattan Project scientists had been troubled by calculations indicating that the detonation might set the whole atmosphere on fire. "For a fraction of a second the light in that bell-shaped fire mass was greater than any ever produced before on Earth. Its intensity was such that it could have been seen from another planet. The temperature at its center was more than 10,000 times that at the Sun's surface. The pressure, caving in the ground beneath, was over 100 billion atmospheres, the most ever to occur at the Earth's surface." [Lansing Lamont, *Day of Trinity*]. On August 6, 8:15 a.m., the US drops "Little Boy" on Hiroshima; on August 9, "Fat Man" destroys Nagasaki. The bombs kill 140,000 in Hiroshima and 80,000 in Nagasaki. Winston Churchill states, "What was gunpowder? Trivial. What was electricity? Meaningless. This atomic bomb is the Second Coming in Wrath." On V-J day in September, World War II ends with 54.8 million dead—twenty-six million in the Soviet Union—predominantly civilians. One third of the world's Jews have been killed in the death camps, including an estimated four million killed with Zyklon B cyanide gas at Auschwitz-Birkenau in southern Poland. In Britain, the civilian death toll from bombing is 51,509. Dylan states, "Behind me, two months when there was nothing in my head but a little Nagasaki, all low and hot" [Lycett]. Returning to London, he works at the BBC—writing, narrating/orating, or otherwise participating in over a hundred programs between December 1945 and May 1949. Arthur C. Clarke first proposes a global system of communications satellites.

1946   Dylan grows more famous. *Deaths and Entrances*, a collection of poems and stories, is published and within a month requires a second printing. On a BBC production, Dylan befriends Richard Burton.

1947   After the Society of Authors awards Dylan a £150 Traveling Scholarship, he and Caitlin and family journey to Italy. In June, the BBC broadcasts Dylan's "Return Journey," written on his visit to Swansea after the 1941 bombing.

1948   Dylan visits Laugharne looking to re-locate there. He takes on scripts for Gainsborough Films, but the company falters. Margaret Taylor, Dylan's patroness, visits Laugharne and eventually buys and provides to the family the Boat House on the estuary of the River Tâf.

1949   Ascending fifty miles above White Sands, New Mexico, a Viking rocket (a German V-2 adapted by Werner von Braun and other German rocket scientists now in the US) achieves the first high-altitude, liquid-fueled rocket flight. Joseph Campbell publishes *The Hero with a Thousand Faces*. In March, Dylan travels to Prague for a few days as guest of the Czechoslovak Writer's Union. In May, with all the Thomases moving to Laugharne, D. J. and Florrie take up residence in The Pelican, a house opposite Browns Hotel, while Dylan, Caitlin, and the children move to the Boat House. In July, Caitlin gives birth to their third child, a second son, Colm.

1950   World population is 2.5 billion. President
           Truman approves development of the
           hydrogen bomb. Stereophonic sound repro-
           duction is introduced. In February, Dylan flies
           to New York and is met at Idlewild airport by
           John Malcolm Brinnin, director of the Poetry
           Center at the 92nd Street Y and organizer of
           Dylan's US tour. After Dylan's performance at
           the Y, E. E. Cummings is so enthused that he
           walks the streets for hours. Dylan meets and
           forms a relationship with Pearl Kazin, a young
           executive with *Harper's Bazaar*. His odyssey
           includes about forty readings and lectures
           throughout the US and Canada. Robert Lowell
           later reported that Dylan spoke much about
           the bombing in World War II. In March, the
           death of Edgar Lee Masters brings to Dylan's
           mind *Spoon River Anthology* with associations
           leading to a radio script on which Dylan is
           working, "The Town That Was Mad," and
           supporting the progress of *Under Milk Wood*. In
           California, in April, he visits Charlie Chaplin
           in Los Angeles, pays an impromptu call on
           Henry Miller in Big Sur, has a taciturn moment
           with Robinson Jeffers at a dinner in Carmel
           Valley, and in San Francisco disconcerts
           Kenneth Rexroth. In June, he returns to Britain
           aboard the *Queen Elizabeth*. Over the summer,
           Pearl writes to Dylan as requested. Caitlin
           effortlessly discovers the letters, writes to
           admonish Pearl, confronts Dylan. In Septem-
           ber, Pearl arrives in London; Dylan meets her,
           and the two share a few days in Brighton.
           Margaret Taylor takes a train to Laugharne to

inform Caitlin about the goings on in London. On return to Laugharne, Dylan finds his marriage seriously askew. In December, *Harper's Bazaar* publishes *A Child's Christmas in Wales*.

1951   The first transcontinental television program is broadcast in the US. *The Catcher in the Rye* by J. D. Salinger is published. While Dylan travels to Persia to develop a film script for the Anglo-Iranian Oil Company, Caitlin writes him that their marriage is over. Dylan maintains contact with Pearl, as Caitlin again discovers. On Dylan's return, he and Caitlin seem to reconcile. Dylan publishes "Do not go gentle into that good night." Brinnin and photographer Rollie McKenna stay at the Boat House in July; the possibility of another American adventure for Dylan is discussed.

1952   The US explodes the first hydrogen bomb on Eniwetok Atoll in the Pacific. In a four- day period, a London smog kills 4,700 persons. Aboard the *Queen Mary*, Dylan and Caitlin embark on his second US tour. Dylan records for Caedmon Records at Steinway Hall on 57th Street, New York. He and Allen Ginsberg share a transient moment. The Thomases return to Britain in May. In November, *The Collected Poems 1934–1952* is published. In December, D. J. Thomas, 76, dies in Laugharne, with his last words, "It's full circle now." After a non-religious ceremony, the body is cremated and buried in Pontypridd, with Caitlin reporting that Dylan was the only mourner attending.

1953   In March, *Collected Poems* is published in the US by New Directions.

Apr 16   Dylan, unaware of his sister's death by cancer in Bombay on the very day, sets sail on the *United States* for his third American tour.

Apr 21   Dylan arrives in New York. Brinnin assigns his associate Liz Reitell to manage the production of *Under Milk Wood*.

May 14   Reitell, Brinnin, and two typists work with Dylan to complete the ending just before actors take the stage. Dylan narrates. Pearl Kazin is in the audience. Afterward, Dylan and Reitell work intensely toward another performance scheduled for the end of the month.

May 20   Dylan meets with Igor Stravinsky in Boston, and they agree "to work on an opera about a man and woman, the only survivors of an atomic catastrophe, rediscovering the physical world around them and having to create a new language and new theories about the origins of the universe" [Lycett].

June 2   Dylan watches the coronation of Queen Elizabeth II. He records for Caedmon.

June 3   He departs for London.

July   At his first session at the Memphis Recording Service of Sun Records, Elvis Presley records two songs reportedly as a gift for his mother.

August   Dylan makes his only television appearance, for the BBC (unpreserved).

Oct 19   Dylan departs for the US a fourth time. He

plans to work in New York for a few weeks, perform *Under Milk Wood* at the 92nd Street Y, and then travel to California to work with Stravinsky. There is some promise of support for his completing his autobiographical piece, *Adventures in the Skin Trade.* He informs Caitlin that he will send for her as soon as he has the money.

Oct 20   Reitell meets Dylan at Idlewild. Experiencing blackouts and chest problems, Dylan uses an inhaler. He and Reitell spend the rest of the day and night together at the Chelsea. After a series of interventions, Dylan makes it through two performances of *Under Milk Wood*, but he collapses afterwards.

Oct 27   Dylan attends a party for his thirty-ninth birthday but is unwell and returns to the Chelsea.

Oct 29   At City College, Dylan performs his last reading.

Nov 2   Air pollution levels threaten those with chest problems, and by the end of the month, over two hundred New Yorkers die from the smog.

Nov 3   Dylan signs a contract for lecture tours at $1,000 a week.

Nov 5   At 2:30 a.m., Dylan is taken from the Chelsea, Room 206, where he has lost consciousness, and is transported, comatose, to St. Vincent's Hospital. Reitell holds a bedside vigil until Caitlin arrives.

Nov 8   Caitlin arrives.

Nov 9   While a nurse is bathing him, **Dylan Thomas dies at 12:40 p.m.** The only other person in the room is John Berryman. The cause of death is vaguely listed as traumatic alcohol abuse. That, along with a mixture of benzedrine, phenobarbitol, atropine, cortisone, and morphine consciously, semi-, and un-consciously consumed or mal-prescribed, seems more accurate.

Nov 13   After a service at the Church of St. Luke-in-the-Fields, attended by E. E. Cummings, Tennessee Williams, and William Faulkner, among others, Caitlin departs with the body on the *United States.*

Nov 25   Dylan is buried in Laugharne, in St. Martin's churchyard.

1954   In January, at the Globe Theater in London, a gala is staged for Dylan, and, on the following day, Richard Burton stars in the first BBC production of *Under Milk Wood.* Caitlin leaves Laugharne to reside in Elba. James Dean, Natalie Wood, and Sal Mineo star in *Rebel Without A Cause.*

1955   In the UK, the term "England and Wales" legally replaces the term "England," and Cardiff is proclaimed the Welsh capital. *Adventures in the Skin Trade* is published.

1956   The Gower Peninsula is officially designated

an Area of Outstanding Natural Beauty, the first in the UK.

1957   Caitlin's book, *Leftover Life to Kill*, is published by Little Brown.

1958   After residing at the Boat House, Florrie Thomas, dies.

1960   World population passes three billion, having tripled in less than a hundred years. Obtained by a bus company, the Swansea and Mumbles Train is dismantled, and its route becomes a promenade and cycle way on the rim of Swansea Bay.

1962   Bob Dylan legally adopts his chosen surname.

1963   Martin Luther King, Jr. proclaims "I have a dream" on the steps of the Lincoln Memorial. In the wake of the Cuban Missile Crisis, a hotline is set up to link White House and Kremlin. Pope John XXIII dies. President Kennedy is assassinated. Shortly before her suicide, Sylvia Plath publishes *The Bell Jar*. The Beatles release "I Want to Hold Your Hand." A film on Dylan Thomas, starring Richard Burton, wins an Academy Award for Documentary Short Subject.

1964   Stanley Kubrick releases *Dr. Strangelove or: How I Learned to Stop Worrying and Love the Bomb*. Arthur C. Clarke checks into the Hotel Chelsea where he and Kubrick develop *2001: A Space Odyssey*. A brass plaque is placed at the hotel entrance:

DEDICATED TO THE MEMORY OF

DYLAN THOMAS

WHO LIVED AND LABORED LAST

HERE AT THE CHELSEA HOTEL

AND FROM HERE

SAILED OUT TO DIE

PRESENTED BY CAEDMON RECORDS

IN COMMEMORATION OF HIS
FIFTIETH BIRTHDAY

OCTOBER 27, 1964

1965   Bob Dylan resides at the Chelsea through late 1966 when *Blonde on Blonde* is released. Resulting from efforts of the Welsh Language Society, Cymdeithias Yr Iaith Gymraeg, Welsh attains equal legality with English, requiring that all road signs and traffic directions in Wales be bilingual.

1967   Marshall McLuhan publishes *The Medium is the Massage*. The Beatles release *Sgt. Pepper's Lonely Hearts Club Band* with an image of Dylan Thomas in the collage on the album cover. Monterey Pop, the first rock festival, is staged at the fairgrounds in Monterey.

1968   Having been launched into space by a Saturn rocket, developed by Werner von Braun, Apollo 8 astronauts—the first to observe the whole Earth from space—broadcast a reading from the Book of Genesis while orbiting the Moon on Christmas Day.

1969   Neil Armstrong steps onto the Moon. With networking of computers at UCLA and Stanford, the internet is created by the Department of Defense. Mother's milk is found to contain four times the amount of DDT permitted in dairy products.

1972   Apollo 17 is the last lunar mission; lacking public interest, three missions are cancelled. Richard Burton, Peter O'Toole, and Elizabeth Taylor appear in a film of *Under Milk Wood*, directed by Andrew Sinclair. For piano credits on Steve Goodman's "Somebody Else's Troubles," Bob Dylan uses the pseudonym Robert Milkwood Thomas.

1974   Scientists report that chlorofluorocarbons are damaging the ozone layer.

1975   Bill Gates and Paul Allen found Microsoft.

1977   Steve Jobs and Steve Wozniak incorporate Apple.

1982   A plaque to Dylan Thomas is unveiled in Poet's Corner, Westminster Abbey.

1984   The term *cyberspace* is introduced by novelist William Gibson. Apple introduces the Macintosh. A sculpture of Dylan by John Doubleday is placed in the Maritime Quarter, Swansea. Doubleday also completes a sculpture of the Beatles for Liverpool.

1985   Scientists discover a hole as large as the US in the ozone layer over Antarctica.

1986   A nuclear reactor at Chernobyl melts down. As radioactive fallout drifts westerly, British sheep farms are blighted—worst off in Wales.

1987   Arthur Miller (another Hotel Chelsea resident) writes in *Timebends,* his autobiography, that "Thomas was making amends by murdering the gift he had stolen from the man he loved" referring to Dylan's father.

1988   George Martin, Beatles producer, releases an album version of *Under Milk Wood,* with portions of dialogue sung to music by Martin and Elton John; Anthony Hopkins plays First Voice. The infrastructure of the internet is opened to commercial users.

1992   Another production of *Under Milk Wood* by George Martin, directed by Anthony Hopkins, features Tom Jones and Catherine Zeta-Jones. The production is staged as "An Evening with Dylan Thomas" for The Prince's Trust and in the presence of HRH Prince Charles, to commemorate the opening of the new AIR Studios at Lyndhurst Hall.

1994   Caitlin Macnamara Thomas dies in Italy, and by her wish, is buried with her husband in Laugharne.

1995   The UN's Intergovernmental Panel on Climate Change confirms global warming. World arsenals contain the potential firepower of 6,000 World War IIs (including the atomic bombs); a single Trident submarine carries warheads with the power of six World War IIs. To host the UK Year of Literature and Writing, Swansea's refurbished and restored Guildhall (built in 1825) opens as The Dylan Thomas Centre, with an address by former US president Jimmy Carter.

1999   About twelve years after surpassing five billion, a UN agency determines October 12 as the approximate day on which world population exceeds six billion.

PILGRIMAGE

Journey to Wales

I was actually uncertain as to why I should be boarding that afternoon Air France flight from San Francisco to Paris, connecting through Amsterdam to Cardiff. The invitation was warm and genuine. Events had been scheduled in Swansea and in Laugharne, and I was bringing my new book of ocean poems. The larger *raison d'être* of the pilgrimage, however, was less clear. Peter had sent me, and I had read, the excellent and recently published biography, *Dylan Thomas: A New Life*, by Andrew Lycett. Also, as recommended by Stan Barkan, I had a few hours before my flight finished reading *Dylan Thomas in America: An Intimate Journal* by John Malcolm Brinnin.

Prior to this, my knowledge of Dylan Thomas had consisted only of the most popular poems, *A Child's Christmas in Wales*, the adoption of his name by Bob Dylan, and an image on the cover of the Beatles album *Sgt. Pepper's Lonely Hearts Club Band* (which, at age sixteen, I had purchased immediately on release). Also in my psyche was an image of Dylan Thomas with a cigarette hanging out of his mouth, and of a few other iconic photographs. I was aware that Dylan had twice visited Monterey and had two encounters with Robinson Jeffers.

Still, I was not exactly sure why I was getting more involved with the life and work of Dylan Thomas. 2008 was not a good year for unnecessary travel expenses. And as if I weren't already edgy enough about life on Planet Earth, I found the stories of Dylan Thomas that I had delved into to be very disturbing. I was much agitated by Brinnin's account, freshly roiling in my mind, of Dylan's dying days and hours in New York.

I passed into and out of needed sleep gliding over Canada, cruising south of Greenland, then arcing on to Paris. I had absolutely no idea what I needed to learn. With the relentless anxieties I had not been able to suppress about the immediate situation of humankind, I felt abjectly dys-empowered to navigate Dylan's life story. But of course, I was grateful for the invite and the opportunity, and I had made the commitment.

The flight proceeded happily, and I felt almost rested at dawn as I glanced out the window to observe Ireland and the British Isles passing below the aileron edge, and then the coast of France. Morning was establishing as I watched the French countryside roll out, punctuated with villages clustered around medieval spires, and then the industrial cities that began to aggregate along the flight path. I was returning from the New World once again to my ancestral continent, land of my forebears, where my name came from. The feeling was tangible, of history arising to embrace and enfold and pull me back and down, as if something in me had never left. I felt the advance of European civilization, Western civilization, in my pulse, the legacy of exploration, expansion, subjugation, subjection, un-civilization, total war. Not a sprinkling of romance, no, not for me, given the overwhelming vertigo of the early 21st century — airborne.

Even so, landed and on the ground, with a surprisingly peaceable layover at Charles DeGaulle airport, I felt composed. Nonchalantly, although American obviously, I made my way through corridors of air-terminal non-locality. Made the KLM hop to Amsterdam where I enjoyed a midmorning interlude and email, then boarded the flight to Cardiff. Through breaks in the cloud-cover, as I observed the English countryside somewhere dissolving into the Welsh, I felt distinctly how it was that I was moving westward again. In fact, my first resonance with the descent to Wales was that I was being drawn—as if a compass magnet—toward the west of things. This attractor stayed with me and grew stronger throughout the trip. I arrived wondering how it was that Dylan Thomas lived his life and brought forth his work at home in Wales, in London, and was also called west, strongly, to the New World in the first half of the last century.

Arrival, Cardiff to Swansea

My fellow passengers bound west from Amsterdam mid-morning, mid-week, seemed to be industrial sales reps or IT engineers, mostly males, returning from the continent. I sensed an earnestness that was as familiar to me as if I were flying home to my native eastern Tennessee. I was called to alertness when the flight attendant presented his speech in vigorous Welsh, and then English. For the first time in my ears, Welsh sounded purely enchanting, and my anticipation was kindled as we made our final approach and landed at Cardiff International.

De-planing, I took in a brace of fresh air, surveyed the tarmac with its spread of quiet jumbo jets, poised for later transoceanic flights I presumed, and proceeded into the terminal. When the commuters peeled off to their separate point of entry, I found myself at times alone in a maze of corridors, welcomed repeatedly by luminous signs in Welsh and English, culminating at a customs booth with a lone (and lonely looking) customs officer. After the routine terse questions about my business in the UK and so forth, I proceeded to baggage claim, where I found Peter exactly as agreed, and we drove off—west to Swansea.

I enjoyed talking with Peter while taking in every detail of the environs that was disclosing itself to me. I was impressed by the bilingual everything and the otherwise, at-first-take, up-to-date vivacity of Welsh life, from the more than ample Cardiff airport to the very smooth traffic flows. I felt a boost of spirit, encouraged, by Peter's welcome, and by the combined cultural and economic forces of the Welsh nation as I beheld them. I simply felt at home on the sceptered isle. The geographical and biographical research I had done was serving me well, and I was giving free reign for the lead character of Dylan Thomas to appear and to instruct me.

But whatever my efforts to focus on the immediate work at hand, I could not escape the larger story that weighed on my shoulders: How do I locate the life and work of Dylan Thomas in this terrifying new century and millennium?

Nonetheless, I felt I was beholding a reset and rebooted Wales—as I had also gathered from reading materials produced by the Welsh Assembly Government in New York, from a plethora of websites, from the luminous surfaces in Cardiff, from the victorious Welsh on every road sign and marker. I felt fresh optimisms laced with the shadows of heavy labors as at last we arrived in Swansea, hometown of Dylan Thomas. I understood the polarity of Swansea: the industrial zone to the east, as we passed through it, the once working harbor area at the middle, and the upscale academic-residential zone to the west and uphill—the Uplands, where Dylan was born.

We drove into the portico of the Marriott at the Marina, the old harbor. I said goodbye to Peter, checked in, found my way upstairs to my room. I was very pleased by the view. There was a new high-rise nearing completion next door, to the east, but to the west, I could look out over the bay—a broad, curving expanse that immediately reminded me of Monterey Bay.

The quest begun, I stepped downstairs and through the lobby to the bar. I was feeling fully intact, copacetic. On the flat screen in the bar, a soccer game—football game—set the mood just fine. I ordered a local brew, Brains SA, to settle my nerves and settle in. Before it arrived, the news streamer across the bottom of the screen began to flash breaking news of attacks in downtown Mumbai. Having traveled in India, my identification with events there was immediate. Suddenly, I felt that Wales was not westerly enough to establish any sense at all of distance from the Eurasian landmass across the Channel. I downed the beer and made my way upstairs to unpack. I never turned on the television in my room during my stay.

I had not brought any romantic fantasies with me to Wales anyway. I had no expectations that this expedition would bring any sort of reverie. I never feel anything *romantic* in my bones anymore, not at this point in my life. That being so, I trusted Peter's itinerary would bring the worthy reckonings, whatsoever they were to be. Our first objective, joining with Robin and Elizabeth in the lobby, was a pub where the youthful Dylan did his early, initiatory drinking—in the nearby locale of Mumbles.

Mumbles

Right off, the name seemed perfect: Mumbles. In Peter's car (a Desire, that is, a model of Citroën), we quickly covered a distance of less than five miles along the rim of Swansea Bay. We parked and stepped up off Oystermouth Road into the bright white, freshly enameled interior of The Antelope and ordered a round—only one round; heavy drinking was not to be our gambit, and Peter was dutiful about the driving.

In this very pub—Peter's emphasis—*much as it is*, the young Dylan found some conviviality. Beer was not only free of taboo, it was, and is, Peter explained, a basic expression for coming of age in the Welsh way, and British way, of fathers and sons. Mother's milk once removed, for all that, I felt. I conjured an image of the tweedy Dylan, in the early 1930s—movie-goer, intern reporter of local color for the *South Wales Daily Post*, venturing the few miles from Swansea to Mumbles, where he had a part (along with his sister Nancy) in a local theater production—standing at the bar. Elevated above the seafront, overlooking the beach, The Antelope was warm and comforting in its handsome state of preservation.

Stepping outside and back down toward the traffic, the wind in our faces, we walked past The Mermaid, another tavern that is much the same as when Dylan was loitering there. Now as then, a pair of voluptuous, ebony mermaids hang emblematic from the cornice over the sidewalk.

But, as I was a little jet-lagged, it was the sweep of the black horizon rimmed with the industrial lights of East Swansea that set the character of my mood as Peter drove us back, Oystermouth Road becoming Mumbles Road, to Victoria Road, to the Marriott.

Such was our convening jaunt.

Swansea Bay

I slept well with the window open as wide as could be to the chill air. Awoke to dawn and my first view of Swansea Beach in broad daylight. I headed downstairs with my laptop under my arm; the wi-fi was in the lobby, as was the latest BBC news on the flat screen. A quick web search revealed that the name Mumbles has nothing to do with a manner of speaking but "is in fact named after the two islands which stand sentinel at the end of the promontory, so called perhaps by the Romans, because of their visual similarity to breasts; *mamma* in Latin and *mammelles* in French." Mythos will out itself. The website explained that the Promenade next to the hotel was in fact the old path of "the first passenger train service in the world, between Swansea and Mumbles, adapted from the transport of limestone to the transport of persons in the year 1807." In 1807, Thomas Jefferson was president. Inspired, I logged off, went upstairs to put on my running gear to trace that historic rail route west toward Mumbles.

I feel that I truly arrive in a given place only when I connect with my feet, jar my bones, register locality in my soft tissues. In a city, I try to connect with the environment in its natural state, to get as close as possible to the original terrain—volcanic rock, glacial deposits, sediments, or however it is that a place had its original being. In Swansea, every morning of my stay, I ran along the Promenade and on the beach toward Mumbles, in the sun and rain, following the vanished tracks of the Swansea and Mumbles Railway, trying to metabolize its whole geology and history. I actively imagined when Swansea Beach had been a gala resort destination.

As mentioned earlier, the expanding curve of the bay reminded me of Monterey. Radically different from Monterey, however, is the extremely gentle slope of the beach into the bay. In my web search, I learned that the tidal ranges of Wales are among the grandest on Earth. This has complicated the problems of pollution in recent centuries. Some intimation of how civilization had gone awry here came to me each morning as I could intuit pervading shadows of the industrial degradation. A lot of work has been done to reverse the damage.

My own obsession, carried with me around the globe, was, and is, atmospheric turbidity. Nowhere on Earth in the 21st century is the sky as blue as it used to be, as I have observed through the decades as I have flown—yes, contributing to the problem. Earth's whole atmosphere is now hazy with aerosol particulates evenly distributed. Dawn has a crystalline whiteness; dusk is smoky, diffused. The colors at sunrise and sunset are not as they once were. This is the universal evidence of our behaviors that are forcing mass extinctions, de-foresting the tropics, drying up rivers, melting the ice sheets, raising sea levels. We are re-arranging the seasons, warping summer, fall, winter, spring. We have destroyed matter, made new elements, re-coded chromosomes, bar-coded molecules, and we are changing night and day. Creation by destruction, more and more, faster and faster. Born after Hiroshima and

Nagasaki, I grew up edgy; in fifteen minutes, as we were warned and as we practiced, the missiles could begin to fall from the sky, bringing the end of everything we knew. The impulse to massive panic attack, planted in me from birth, has never gone away. Now the timing has gone from fifteen minutes to already-too-late. What is the matter with us? Can we stop ourselves from destroying ourselves, despoiling life on Earth? Why do we have this much power? Even if I never see it, can the sky be pure blue, again? Yes, it must be so. Are we going to be able to turn this around? Isn't everybody noticing?

That's how my thoughts were shaped as I ran. That's how they are always shaped as I run; no place to hide. Nonetheless, a few miles along, I had enough oxygen to free my mind for the present moment, wonderful moment. I had begun to love Swansea, Mumbles, from the ground up. Jogging out of jetlag, leaving my footprints in the wet sand, taking in the shore-places of Dylan the boy, I was ready for adventure and for the return, the recursive spiral into my own British ancestry and cultural heritage. Running the path of the old rails and back, I succeeded at recognizing the pristine topography as the Romans and Vikings found it, and as the Celtic and Paleolithic tribes lived it here in the country of Wales—or, in Welsh, Cymru, Kŭm'ree. Keeping up my pulse rate, I was ready to contact the spirit of Dylan Thomas.

I scanned the horizon as far as I could toward the Bristol Channel. Then, closer, a large, distinctively corrugated, oddly frilly shell, an oyster shell, unlike any I had seen before, caught my eye. I stopped and picked it up, examined it. The shell was very dense. I carried it back to the hotel and placed it before my open window, a talisman.

Gower

Showered, dressed, and quickly seated in the hotel restaurant, I was served a much bigger breakfast than I bargained for, poached haddock, eggs sunny side up, and lots and lots of plain toast. Found Robin and Liz by the front desk, and Peter appeared at the door, ready and able to lead us onward.

For our first full outing, the destination was Gower—something of a nature preserve, I gathered. Leaving Swansea, we meandered northwestward on a winding road, edged here and there with stone houses, vine-laden and shaded, all tangled in my mind. Still a little jet-lagged, I was never clear about the actual boundaries of Gower—perhaps there aren't any, precisely. What a thoroughly Welsh name, I felt, Gower—a strange and intriguing attractor.

At every turn in Wales I was aware that our immediate experience in the first decade of the 21st century is laid over dark sediments of 20th-century life that were always directly in evidence, and in turn had been laid atop 19th- and 18th-century strata, and deeper, unfathomable strata. These layers are somewhat indicated by the Welsh names, signs, and significations. I felt no separating of name from place in Wales—every Welsh term seeming to carry some suggestion of lore. Interestingly, however, I did not hear Welsh during my whole stay. Dylan Thomas did not speak or write in Welsh, but he heard plenty of it.

The entwined ravines gave way to rolling mounds and meadows, wild grasses and reeds. I was suddenly aware that I was on an island, the largest of the British Isles—a quantum shift of awareness, proprioceptive, of all the stories, of Shakespeare and Company, Robin Hood, Old Mother Goose, all of British literature, everything, accordingly. The known facts of my linguistic-literary inheritance took on a differently felt emotion. I sensed the geophysical detachment from the Continent—more primordial than the cultural and psychological distinctions. I also felt again, a little bit dizzying, the westerly motion, the gazing to the west with restlessness, drawing me toward the horizon where the sun goes down, to the night sea.

Even in its undefined wildness, Gower seemed small and vulnerable, particularly so in contrast with the Pacific expanses of the central coast of California, from where my consciousness was still being transferred. And yet, even in the wide open spaces of the American West, I have grown to accept that any perception of a particular landscape as "relatively undisturbed" carries with it the reality of "granted reprieve." In other words, the question is, how drastically has the natural state of any given place been altered by human activities and intentions?—since there is no place on Earth that remains unaffected by humanity. The experience of any locality must be placed on a dys-continuum from less-disturbed to most-grievously disturbed.

I wondered how the Welsh managed Gower. I wondered how this locality could have survived as intact as it seemed to be, what powers of property and what governing bodies granted the place reprieve through recent centuries. Among the mounds and meadows, we came upon a herd of Welsh ponies roaming without fences. Charming, that's the word, and hardy. Of a size somewhere between ponies as I have known and a small horse, they seemed to prevail where they grazed. Welsh ponies, wild and woolly; I was very curious about them. How consoling, alleviating, I felt their presence to be.

There were no difficulties for me grasping the specific and wild grandeur of what I beheld. It seems to me all the poetry of the British Isles derives some resonance from the forces of such fields. I got that as I had never gotten it—of origin, archaic, magical, mythical. But these perceptions did not become cinematic. Something distinctly Welsh about the place reserved itself as pre-cinematic, unfilmed, or unfilmable, hidden from the gaze of the wider world.

Peter stated our specific destination to be Worms Head, on the western tip of the Gower Peninsula.

Worms Head

Nearing the tip of the peninsula, the narrow road tumbled into the village of Rhossili; more power in a name. The stone houses seemed ancient, as well they may be, some of them forming the actual edges of the roadway. I felt a quietening, some distanciation from the 21st century. I wondered who might have the opportunity or fate to live in such houses. Finally, the road widened into a lot where we parked beneath the broad horizon and set out on a narrow footpath.

To the right, a cliff fell precipitously for a thousand feet or so. The opening vista disclosed a long beach below, curving north and west. An immediate resonance for me was with the Big Sur coast. Here was another west coast, headlands plunging down to golden sand, surmounted by large breakers white-maned with spindrift. I took in a deep breath and felt at home.

I connected with the young Dylan, here, where all youth begins and dwells for a while and is lost and begins again. Thus the sonority in the name D. J. and Florrie chose for their son—a name now propagated very widely. Dylan is Welsh for *sea* or *ocean*, and by extension in the character of Welsh myth, the name is *son of a sea wave*.

At what depths do we find the collective memory of our sea life? Jeffers speaks of the *tides in our veins*. Brine into blood was the primordial transubstantiation. What is held beneath the surface, invisibly, on the oceanic horizon, is held also, unfathomably, within us. This is true as true can be, as we have learned to stand and breathe, as we have crawled out and climbed up, carrying our dreams to the apex of noon. And it is possible, perhaps for most all of us, to stand at the water's edge and to feel Origin, some archaic sense of closure, as the waves arise and collapse world without end, amen.

There we stood, our small entourage, observing the brightness of day at the gate of the trail leading farther out to the formation named Worms Head. Strong winds blew time away. A field of sheep grazed in pastoral splendor, with a sign warning *turistas* that those harassing the sheep might more or less be shot, as I read it, at the will of the shepherd. Another sign warned that if the tide is coming in, any sensible person should venture no farther out; no assurances that an emergency helicopter could arrive in time to redeem a miscalculation.

Peter spoke of the treks of Dylan Thomas and his youthful companions, sometimes walking the fifteen miles from Swansea to Worms Head. I could visualize the power of this place for them. I also remembered that, unlike Jeffers, Dylan wrote hardly anything about seascape-in-itself apart from human predications and predicaments. That was how Dylan found himself.

We turned and retraced our steps the way we had come and found ourselves in the tavern at Worms Head Inn, quiet as a chapel. After an hour with appropriate libations, we turned back through Rhossili and enjoyed again the length of the peninsula. We had work coming up in Swansea.

The Dylan Thomas Centre, Swansea

After transition time—Peter always set a moderate, effective pace—we drove from the hotel the short distance to downtown. Swansea, I had read, has been continuously inhabited for a thousand years. The streets evoke old pathways laid down prior to industrialization. We wound the short distance toward the Marina and parked beside a boldly handsome, three-story building of Palladian architecture—the Dylan Thomas Centre. My feeling was that of walking into an old post office: masses of masonry, hardwood door frames and banisters, a lot of brass here and there, a chamber of echoes. Peter explained that the building was the old Guildhall. He showed us the well-outfitted lecture room where we were to perform that evening. In the homey gift shop circled with original black-and-white photographs of Dylan and various locales, we had tea and Welsh cakes along with introductions to the good people who run the place. We then made our ways, each on our own, to the quadrant of the first floor that is the actual exhibition area.

Through the entrance, I turned left and perused the list of patrons, including Sir Paul McCartney and William

Jefferson Clinton. My thoughts were, first off, how it is that celebrity affirms all. How interesting that the image of Dylan Thomas in the collage on the cover of *Sgt. Pepper's*—arguably the best known album cover in history—should validate the poet, his life, work, all. Of course, the image is there to honor the authentic influence of Dylan Thomas of Swansea on Lennon and McCartney of Liverpool. And along with a few poems in high school English Lit, that collage image had been my first connection with Dylan. Of course, an image of Bob Dylan of Duluth, Minnesota, is also in that collage. I wondered if Sir Paul had ever stood where I stood. I doubted Bob Dylan had.[1] Many famous personages probably had stood at that spot, including perhaps some of the cast of the recently completed film about Dylan and Caitlin, *The Edge of Love*, with Keira Knightly. I could imagine the footsteps of busloads of schoolchildren treading past; perhaps, because of the subject matter, these are students in their teen years. And otherwise I felt the convergence of worldwide interests.

The legacy of Dylan Thomas has been embraced in his native land, his hometown, the centre. I noted the similarity of style with the Steinbeck Center in Salinas, California. Clearly, there are conventions of exhibit design. In Swansea, as well as Salinas, the quest to engage the broadest possible demographic spectrum of visitors brings about easy-to-navigate displays, narrative sequences, entertaining features, interactive devices. All can serve educational purposes, no doubt. The downside, depressing as I felt it, is the homogenizing effect of translating this-author-and-that, this-history-and-that, into a lowest common visual-auditory vernacular. I felt a little wary about how the life and times of Dylan Thomas were going to be channeled through these interpretive frames.

Still, I was more than ready and eager to learn more about the whole-life that I expected to be portrayed. I was glad to gain multi-sensory information.

For use in the poetry workshop that Robin and I were set to lead, I jotted down some introductory quotes of Dylan stenciled on the walls:

> Poetry is what makes me laugh or cry or yawn, what makes my toenails twinkle.
> —Poetic Manifesto 1951

> I wanted to write poetry in the beginning because I had fallen in love with words . . . I cared for the colors the words cast on my eyes . . .

> It is the record of my individual struggle from darkness toward some measure of light.

Straightforward. Accessible. Other, more daring quotes were stenciled at various stops and junctures farther on as I drifted here and there around the chamber.

A glass case held a painting by the juvenile Dylan. I enjoyed the intimacy of access to those pigments and brushstrokes, but I could discern no particular signal of emergent genius in that medium.

A television screen showed black-and-white footage from the 1950s in New York. In a repeating loop, Barbara Cohen and Marianne Roney tell about their founding of Caedmon Records with Dylan's sessions at Steinway Hall on West 57th Street, across from Carnegie Hall, inventing all at once the genre of spoken-word records. This is part of how Dylan became the world's first media-star poet. Other footage tells of the New York productions of *Under*

Milk Wood in the final chapter of Dylan's life. The stories seem best told as they are in black-and-white, as if the world depicted was in fact a world of black, white, and shades of gray. When I was a child, that's the way history was. Watching these loops, it seemed to me the temperature fell.

Winding farther round, I came upon the wide, wooden doors, from Dylan's Writing Shed. This panel was removed in the restoration of that structure, which now stands near the Boat House in Laugharne. Through this actual threshold passed the very man to face his duties at the writing table.

In a room off to the side of the main hall, a screen shows clips from *The Edge of Love*, adding a Technicolor, cinemaesthetic dimension to the saga. Enclosed in plexiglass cases are the costumes, the shoes, worn by Keira Knightly as Vera Phillips, Sienna Miller as Caitlin, Matthew Rhys as Dylan—the facsimile lives. Unwieldy, for me; I felt like I had gotten lost in a swirling hall of mirrors. The film has not been released in the US, is not available on Netflix. I don't know why.[2]

Also in the auxiliary room, on a wall behind a pane of glass, hangs a linen tablecloth, preserved over fifty years after an Algonquinesque dinner occasion with Dylan and Caitlin and another couple in some New York City restaurant. The tablecloth is covered with four drawings, one in pencil or ink by each member of the party. One of the other couple was a trained artist, and the figure shows it. The other three drawings are unremarkable, infantile it seemed to me. One is angrily scratched over. I recall that Caitlin did a lot of drawing when she joined her husband on the second American tour in 1952. Party stains, blood stains, all the same it seemed to me—the look of a shroud. I moved on.

Back in the main room, I flitted around a little more rapidly, feeling the final chapters of *Dylan Thomas In America* tightening in my chest. One more screen appeared with another loop of black-and-white footage—of the funeral in Laugharne. Disconcerting. I gazed intently at the scene, of a nature deeply familiar to me from the many funerals in the southern Appalachian hills of my childhood. In heavy black coats, faces stunned and weary, the solemn assembly march unevenly, down the sloping churchyard.

Peter walked up behind me, "There's Caitlin; you can see her there."

Yes, I looked to see the images of Caitlin, staggering, barely able to stand, assisted by those on either side of her, lifting her up from under her arms. I wondered who all the figures were. Almost unbearable it was to watch this all closing in. I watched it again. Again. The end.

I turned to leave, returned as I was, after the whole life, to the entrance, and there I noted the bronze bust. I think I had noticed it coming in. A bust of Dylan. I looked more closely, stepped up to it. The eyes are closed. I read the plaque. A death mask.[3] It rang me to the bones, absolutely, this artifact, this furnishing. I got very close, examining the complexion of the man, in death, Dylan.

What came to my mind was the first death mask I directly observed, that of Frederic Chopin, in a museum on the island of Mallorca, decades ago. Oddly, I also recalled a bizarre happening in my life, in San Francisco, at the DeYoung Museum, when I stood alone and face to face with the golden mask of Tutankhamen for about twenty minutes. Tut's eyes are wide open, Dylan's and Chopin's are closed. Three death visages, and upon all three, I gazed as steadily as I could. The *materia* did not yield any secrets. Of course, with the death masks of Chopin and Dylan, I could examine the actual character of their faces. The horrifying stories of Dylan's final hours in New York began to well up inside me as I looked more and more closely into the very pores, trying to read something of the events in that fateful room at the Chelsea in Manhattan, the final path to St. Vincent's, that room where he breathed his last.

Too much. Too much.

It was time for us to go, time to make a break, transition, back to the hotel for a while.

A few hours later, the workshop at the centre, with good poets from *The Seventh Quarry* community, went very well. The evening event, the readings by Robin and me, also went well. In the audience was Aeronwy Thomas who had caught a train from London to trek with us. Afterward, we climbed to the bar on the second floor. All went well. Not a late evening because the next morning Aeronwy was going with us to Fern Hill and on to Laugharne.

The Drive to Fern Hill

The five of us packed into the Desire and headed out of Swansea. The highway system looked new and seemed efficient. Suburban Swansea appeared reasonably cogent. The farther we drove, the more I wondered how the words of Dylan Thomas might be faring in the day-to-day life of the first generation coming of age in the 21st century.

We made a stop at Tesco so that Peter could procure batteries for his digital camera. As the rest of us waited, I observed mid-morning customers arriving, crowding into checkout lines, pushing heavy-laden grocery baskets through the lot. In those carts were, I supposed, the usual makings of traditional Welsh breakfasts, lunches, dinners; household stuff; the British economy transported one basket at a time. No observable difference between Tesco and my neighborhood Safeway 5300 miles to the west.

My mind veered. How does it all work? Where does the food come from? Where does the water to grow the food come from? How does the global economy produce sponge-mops and dishwashing liquid, razor blades and batteries, and the hundred billion things? Where does the garbage go? How is the free market economy as we know it going to be sustainable, for ever and ever? These questions and more escalated as I wondered about the accelerating collapse of the global financial system, desertification, severing ice shelves. Surrounded by dark black asphalt and rows of cars between lightposts freshly planted, I could not figure anything out—never can— feeling increasingly alarmed, dissociated, dense. Peter brought back the batteries. We cornered into a queue for petrol. I thought about the North Sea oil rigs. I took a deep breath, settled into my seat, vowed to un-furrow my brow, enjoy present company, and take in the discovery of Carmarthenshire, the land of Merlin.

Our route soon opened unto verdant, rolling hills laced with hedgerows and dotted with sheep. The sky was spotted with puffy clouds as I searched for pure blue. The Welsh hills are a lot like Tennessee hills, but there is a distinctive character to Carmarthenshire. I was tuning in Thomas Hardy, thinking how Hardy's Wessex was not far from where we were. Both Dylan Thomas and Robinson Jeffers were drawn to Hardy's settings and characters at the death of an age.

Aeronwy's grandfather and grandmother Thomas both had roots in Carmarthen. They were contemporaries of my grandparents, who were subsistence farmers, all of them, in rural Southern Appalachia. Aeronwy's father was born in industrial Swansea in 1914; my father was born in 1916 in the country, raised there. These facts were in my mind as we drove deeper into the woods. I directly related to Dylan in his day, traveling on train, bus, a hired car, to visit his un-citified relations. Aeronwy has country stories, and we talked a little about that.

Peter knew exactly where we were going, branching off the main road, then continuing slowly up a shady lane.

Fern Hill

Nearing the crest, we parked on the left and walked upward. We hardly spoke. A heavy iron gate appeared in a stone wall on the right, and on a vine-entwined pillar, I made out distinct, burgundy script: Fern Hill. Beyond the gate stood a substantial manor house[4] and outbuildings as if lifted off the classic edition of *The Wind in the Willows*. This was Toad Hall, matter-of-factual.

After a moment, I walked farther up, turned around and gazed down on the scene. I was standing under a massive tree with branches forming a thickly plaited canopy. As morning sunlight animated the limbs, I registered raindrops falling into my face, a real shower. This seemed miraculous—a bright, clear morning with a rain shower falling only in this one exact place. Consecrating.

I called down to the others, "It's raining here under this tree!"

Liz called out, "It's hoar frost melting."

Well, of course, that's what was happening. But the explanation did not alter the enchantment. Heavy drops were still falling on my face and shoulders—a personal drenching. The falling drops were musical, persistently ringing as they fell, tinkling bells.

In the trailing plants along the stone wall, a small bird darted. I am a lover, not a scholar, of birds. This one looked exotic, unlike any bird I had ever seen before: small, intensely and also softly russet-colored, difficult to describe. I studied it. My mind began to work. "Here is a beautiful little bird," I spoke. And just as my thought was advancing, Aeronwy, who had walked up beside me, spoke what my brain had nearly figured out: "It's a robin." Aha! I realized I was beholding for the first time in my life an English robin. Grace on wings, a pure gift, and no-nonsense, too. The sighting triggered some childhood memory (wonderland mode) long dormant. I recalled an illustration from a very early book where a colorful robin appeared, but young as I was, I could not reconcile the image in the book with the robins in the backyard in Tennessee. This busy robin brought an epiphanic difference. From that moment, Fern Hill was transfiguring.

Aeronwy began to relate some of the family lore rooted like the tree we were standing under—names and characters. Her telling was lively and lyrical. Some of the details woven through various beats and measures evoked knowledge I had gotten through my studies. I listened alertly and, naturally, felt more present to Fern Hill than her father's poem had brought me. Aeronwy's stories warmed everything and grounded my quest for the long, slow history of the place.

Thus beheld, before us, Fern Hill. How grateful I was. Walking downhill toward the car, to my right, abruptly, I heard and looked down and sighted below the bluff a full running brook, as Dylan sang it:

And the sabbath rang slowly
In the pebbles of the holy streams.

Anew, I realized where I was. *Fields high as the house* . . .
tunes from the chimneys . . . Before my eyes those very
chimneys, and behind and beyond them, the fields rising.
A total grok. *Vision splendide.* Spinning. Spellbinding.

Fern Hill to Laugharne

What I could not tell you yet, dear Reader, is that high above Fern Hill looms a massive steel tower with high-voltage transmission lines slung through the sky. Yes, I was stunned. I didn't utter a single word. I imagined there had been a fierce battle, surely, against this desecration, but I didn't have the heart to ask. The sight of those power lines plunged me back into the maw of paradox, my fissile brain. No release from self-implication, no denying I expected to plug in my laptop later at the hotel. Electrical transmission is no respecter of persons or properties or poetic sentiments. How could I pretend it to be otherwise? Have met enemy, is us. Anyway, and likewise, the saga of Fern Hill, the poem itself, is not all romantic paradise, young and easy. Followed all the way through the final stanza, the poem ends tangled up, complexed. There's nothing simple about that poem, I'd say.

And so it was. Peter turned the car around and rolled back down the lane into the land of legends and lost peasantries, dreaming the myth onward. I was alert to the antecedent and indigenous. Nearing Johnstown, a glimpse of a starkly Non-conformist church building reminded me of Dylan's wider experiences on his sojourns to the holy streams and the sun all day. I imagined the boy plucked out of his rural dreams and driven, a wagon drawn by Welsh ponies perhaps, to fill his designated twitching place on a pew. Lycett describes the sermon style in that "tight-knit Welsh-speaking world" as *hwyl*—full-sail. *Hwyl*. Similar howls were engraved in my genes in a country church in Sawmill Holler in Tennessee. *Hwyl*— coiled in and springing out of Dylan's elocution. A familiar quiver for me.

Onward, it seemed I was uncoding more of the rural landscape, sensing the hauntings of ancestral generations. I could sense the successful strivings of recent centuries, the establishment of the Industrial Age, the parting of the psychic seams as young people left the glens for mining towns and cities. As we drove, I felt further twistings back through time, retrieving the Celtic strains of yore, among us still, and deeper down into pre history. Simultaneously, the modern biographies we were pursuing spiraled forth, the intrigues of Dylan and Caitlin. Whatsoever was becoming whatsoever is, back and forth, like the sea waves, arriving and departing all at once, always.

As we neared our destination, I felt vortices, powers, principalities, paradoxes, as strung and sung by the bard of Cwmdonkin. The Great Attractors, self-organizing, dys-organizing, loose-tight, led to Laugharne—core and sinew, marrow, stains.

Writing Shed

Laugharne is a small, medieval village set at the edge of a
large tidal basin at the mouth of the River Tâf. Two- and a
few three-story buildings define the narrow streets as a
small maze. Aeronwy was energized by her birthplace and
childhood home. Peter also was charged by our arrival. As
we wound through, Peter pointed out a structure at the
center of things, The Pelican, residence of Dylan's parents
for a stint, and where his father died. Across the street
from it, Browns Hotel, a center of social life at-large for
Dylan and Caitlin, each and both. Peter said we would
return to these sites later, after our afternoon readings.

We passed a small parking lot. Above it peaceably
loomed the stonework of Laugharne Castle. I had
glimpsed Swansea Castle also, and the link between the
two carried me to the time of the Norman Conquest when
both Swansea and Laugharne were equally vulnerable to
sea invaders. Peter drove forward between a cluster of
houses clinging to the bluff and dropped us off in the
middle of a neighborhood. Then Aeronwy took the lead as
we strode briskly along a paved driveway, tree-lined and
shaded. All that I knew about our day in Laugharne was

that we were reading our poems at the Boat House. I was also aware how important it was to be on time because provisions had been made for tea following the reading.

A bright and quickening day it continued to be. Everything seemed in very good order, well-kept, as we walked on. I noted a small garage ahead, on the right. As we neared, I'm not sure who said it, I think it was Aeronwy who stopped and made a brief remark, but there it was, a sight to behold: the Writing Shed of Dylan Thomas. What hit me right away was how it was a typically male domain—woodshed, tool shed, writing shed. It is a one-car garage with a gabled roof, pretty plain and simple; the wood trim is painted a faintly aquamarine hue (same as the trim at Fern Hill), including the double doors; the door on the right has a window.

As we approached, I could see more clearly how the structure extends over the cliff-ledge, on stilts, as Dylan was fond of saying. Aeronwy forged on ahead of us. Peter, having caught up, reminded me that the existing structure is a restoration of the original (its front doors on display at the centre in Swansea). I stepped forward and looked into the interior, meticulously re-creating, I presumed, the original milieu, with original furnishings, and the complete contents arranged/disarranged as Dylan left them well over a half-century ago. That is the intended effect.

At the end opposite the doors, beneath double windows, curtained, stands a sturdy, wooden kitchen table, his desk, with a sturdy, armless, wooden chair pushed back, and another, non-matching chair at the right. The desk has a globed oil lamp and papers scattered about. Surrounding the windows, tacked on the wall, are multiple images: Blake. Whitman. Auden. Edith Sitwell.

The young Yeats, I thought. Several others. An image of D. H. Lawrence is central. Above it, at the apex of the ceiling is a portrait of the younger Dylan himself. A sensuous Modigliani hangs among multiple lithographs hither and thither.

I gathered my impressions quickly, not much time to process. The perch is jarring, the more I thought about it. Even with a small fireplace, it was most often cold and damp inside, as I had read; Dylan didn't have tremendous affection for his man-space. Yet it was his. The only other space I've read about that he precisely called his own was his bedroom on Cwmdonkin Drive. There is something of the feeling of a teenager's room to the shed, everything strewn around, posters of heroes on the walls. A place of escape, refuge, exile, boredom, moods, fantasy, work. Entrapment? By what? By whom?

At that desk he wrote as he wrote, draft after draft, assiduously, excruciatingly, meticulously "at glacial speed" as he put it, with extreme care to realize his flamboyance. Toward the end of his life, as at the beginning, he rendered some of the most powerfully influential literary works of the 20th century.

Boat House: Terrace and Harbour

Brinnin's journal includes the telling about his very brief stay at the Boat House. He details one night as the younger children trotted upstairs at bedtime. As I had emailed Aeronwy, I still felt Brinnin's text, decades after the fact, to be oddly invasive; a little weird it seemed to be visiting her childhood without her consent. She made nothing of that comment, having adjusted to a lifetime of endless attentions to her family, I figured. (At one point, I asked her when it was that she first was aware of her father's fame. She said it was when an anonymous scholar from Michigan showed up to visit for a few days; she didn't care for him and dispatched him effectively, as she recounts in *A Daughter Remembers Dylan*.)

Many such ideas and more complicated ones were pressing in, crowding my mind on the short path connecting Writing Shed to the family abode. Aeronwy explained how the walk had been leveled and paved to accommodate the many thousands of tourists who visit annually. She pointed how radically adventurous the approach had been in her childhood. Now, as then, the path fishhooks around the three-story structure and leads

down steps, once much more perilous, to the front door.
And thus, we arrived.

Navigating inside, sorting through the several pre-
existing texts in my mind. The interior spaces were alive
with the energies and activities of those who had
congregated for the afternoon event. Some had come to
greet Aeronwy, that was clear, and to hear her read, as
well as Robin and me. There were those who maintained
the site, those who cared for the gift shop (the former
bedroom of Aeronwy's older brother, Llewelyn). Several
people were in the small kitchen (every room is small on a
pre-modern scale) preparing the tea. The whole situation
was alert and busy. Very Welsh it felt.

We made way, Aeronwy conversing with all,
confirming that, given the clear skies, we might stage our
reading outside; yes, that would be okay, and best, was the
consensus. Thus the whole party was promptly transferred
out the back door and onto the terrace where a few were
already relaxing around tables in the sunshine. The
immediate task for Robin and me was to locate ourselves
and set out our books. That done, I began to take in the
environment.

Standing at the wall of the terrace, the sweeping vista
of the River Tâf, Afon Tâf, estuary spread broadly to the
horizon, muddy at low tide. The river itself was running
adjacent to the house, hooking toward Laugharne and then
outward toward the open sea, in the general direction of
Ireland. I wondered about the health of the mud, the river,
the environment upstream. I wondered if anyone still
gathered cockle fish, as Caitlin had done.

To the west across the estuary extends a small
peninsula, the mound set forth for all time in Dylan's
poem "Over Sir John's hill." To the east across the estuary

is the far node of the ferry that once ran across the Afon Tâf to the landing at the Boat House. Via that ferry, at age nineteen, Dylan first arrived in Laugharne, to his immediate enchantment. Fourteen years after he first sighted the place, Dylan's patroness, Margaret Taylor, provided it to them, for him to write and for Caitlin and family.

The terrace above the harbour is of recent construction, the result of substantial community efforts to shore up the property. It took me a while to reconcile the vision before me with the photo of the same spot when it consisted only of a small wooden deck. On that deck, Dylan and Brinnin were photographed by Rollie McKenna, the New York photographer who accompanied Brinnin in 1952. The photograph is on the back cover of Brinnin's book. That exact spot turned out to be the setting for our reading. We faced the house, and the folks inside came out the back door from kitchen and living room and assembled.

Peter introduced Aeronwy. She read two of her father's poems: "And Death shall have no dominion" and "The force that through the green fuse drives the flower." Then she read poems from her book *Burning Bridges*. Robin read from his book, *Unbidden Angel*, and I from mine, *Rivulets of Light: Poems of Point Lobos and Carmel Bay*, a few poems sea to sea. The event came off as well as the one in Swansea. It was bliss for me—at the focal point of that vortex with many worlds converging before my eyes and in my heart.

Perfectly on time for tea.

Boat House: Tea

The assembly dissolved and, as many as could fit, re-congregated inside. Aeronwy went into the living room, and the occasion was properly observed. Robin, Liz, and I stayed outside with the stacks of books and conversed with those who were in no hurry. I further absorbed the scene and the situation as the northerly, late November light began slightly to fade. I drifted around, had a moment in the tiny toilet attached to the house, as Dylan had not failed to describe. I stepped into the stairway well between kitchen and living room for a quick look inside, warmly consanguine.

The kitchen, very compact, was supplying the living room with platters of square picnic sandwiches (egg and cress, cheese and pickle, on white bread, crusts trimmed away), and Welsh cakes. Aeronwy was holding court with the folks at main and side tables. The wall away from the entry had a display rack with a complete collection in several rows of richly colored plates. I recalled reading that Caitlin had great affection for bright ceramics. Ceramic bowls, pitchers, and other pieces sat here and there in the room. I doubted that these were the everyday sort that

were, in tense moments, hurled. The sandwiches and tea were stocked on a narrow table under the window looking out on the terrace.

I stepped back outside into the light more definitely dimmed. I flashed again on the back cover of *Dylan Thomas In America,* Rollie McKenna's shot of Dylan in his native garb, foot propped on a chair, with Brinnin dressed in a prim, tailored suit, sitting on the railing, a pot of tea on the table in front of them. In that spot where we read, Liz and Robin were conversing with two Welsh gentlemen, locals, who were telling their own stories of places and times as they used to be. Taken up by the rhythms of their speech, I was happily enough unable to discern every inflection or capture every name they mentioned. Their gab, their garb, and their gestures were of a whole piece—and they were assuredly disposed to do exactly as they were doing and to sing right there and then their odes and laments. I felt welcomed, allowed, and old, and sad along with them. Grateful to be alive and where I was, even while obsessing about atmospheric turbidity.

The Welshmen had spoken all, and they and most of the others had departed when we gathered inside. Our party of five sat at the table where Caitlin and Dylan had dined, in the ceramic glow, downing more tea. Talking another moment, after the morning drive through Carmarthenshire, the moment at Fern Hill, the afternoon, afterglow. At a pause in the conversation, I pulled out the New Directions paperback with **Dylan Thomas** *Collected Poems* in large black font, the classic black-and-white cover that appeared on half the college dorm shelves of the late 60s and early 70s. I had brought it from California in my backpack. The moment had come. I asked each of the others to sign the book, and they did. And otherwise,

done, Peter urged us on. We had enough daylight for a very important stop: the gravesite.

Peter, Liz, and Robin departed. I kept back with Aeronwy, who had goodbyes with the keeper of the day, and general goodbyes. I was trying to imagine how it might be for Aeronwy leaving her childhood home after such an occasion. After I had carried into the kitchen a couple of platters of surplus sandwiches, a good chap returned with a large brown sack that he had stuffed full of them, and Welsh cakes too, crisply wrapped in foil. There was nothing else to do but stow the sack in my backpack, and so I did.

Aeronwy was still finishing up when she came to fetch me from the living room and proceed toward the front door we had come in a few hours earlier. Then, her voice clear as a bell, she inquired, "Did you get a chance to look around upstairs?"

To which, I responded, "No, no. Actually, I didn't."

"Well," she said, "let's take a quick look round."

Boat House: Parlour

In my early thirties, I had the freedom, as poet-in-residence, of many quiet hours in Tor House, home of Robinson and Una Jeffers, in Carmel. The house and tower had just been purchased from Jeffers' descendants by the foundation dedicated to preserving the property. And more than two decades later, I unexpectedly found myself, as Aeronwy guided, having a few quiet moments upstairs in the Thomas family quarters. Jeffers, Dylan, and Caitlin were together once, in Carmel Valley, on Dylan's second American tour. Dylan and Jeffers had already met in Carmel on Dylan's first tour when he had traveled to the West Coast alone. By all accounts, the dinner with the three of them and several others was not an ordinary cup of tea. Dylan and Caitlin stormed out of the room in a raging argument, shortly to return as if absolutely nothing had happened.

Like Tor House now, the interior of the Boat House has, no doubt, been shaped by the idealizations of those tasked with maintaining and presenting the landmark to unending streams of visitors. Why is it that people come to these shrines? What is it we are looking for? Maybe some psychic residues of all of us visitors, our quests, our fantasy-projections into celebrity, our dreams, steadily infuse the walls of such heritage sites.

I followed Aeronwy up the narrow staircase that bisects the whole house from first to third floors. On the second story, we stood at the door of the parlour, Caitlin's parlour shall we say. The hearth at the center caught my eye. My mind flashed on the hearth in Una Jeffers' studio in Hawk Tower, where, engraved in a wooden mantel, is a key phrase: *Ipsi Sibi Somnia Fingunt.* "For themselves they shape their own dreams"—a line from Virgil. I had found Tor House to be The American Dream House. Archetypal. It came to me that the Boat House might be equivalently The Welsh Dream House of the same epoch.

Dylan was nineteen years old, making his first visit to Laugharne, when he eyed and immediately selected the Boat House as dream house. Later, he and Caitlin met for the first time in Laugharne. As I looked around the parlour, I had the feeling of it being a playhouse, her fortress. I thought about the younger Irish girl dancing on tabletops, the strident young woman already living her life to the full on the day she and Dylan crossed paths. And soon they got married, and in a couple of years were living in Laugharne. And within a decade or so were at home with their three children in the Boat House. They did shape this dream for themselves, it would seem.

We shape our dreams, our dreams shape us. A foundation must be laid, or stilts put in place. A life-world must be altered, points by particles, semi-permanently. Regions must be separated on different sides of various planes. Boundaries divide exteriors from interiors where objects—with their own outsides and insides—can then be placed. Pitchers and bowls, ovens. Chests of drawers, beds. Furniture.

A parlour is an interior space set apart and furnished for parlance, parleys, and parables. And for the purposes of deliberately blurring fantasies and actualities in impressive and civilized ways. Whence cometh the magic and murkiness of parlours. By my projection, or otherwise, the Boat House parlour felt strained. Two overstuffed chairs faced each other conversationally on either side of the hearth. On a squat stool in the corner to my left sat the wood-veneered radio that the BBC gave to the Thomas family so that they could listen to Dylan's programs. I could imagine the children summoned, seated, hearing their dad's disembodied voice beamed from afar. Did they comprehend that his voice was filling so many other parlours in Wales, in Great Britain?

Where we stood, I reckoned, was the center of the whole house, in three dimensions. My mind projected a 3D model: below us the living room; next door to it, the kitchen; behind us the bedroom used by Llewelyn; above his room, the youngsters' room; directly above us, the conjugal bedroom. Thus were the family dreams concretized in solid geometry. This was the domestic receptacle, the dwelling place, the container. Thus was the Welsh economy exemplified, once upon a very particular time, and one set of fantasies made manifest somehow.

Turning to follow her out, I was going ask Aeronwy how she felt about her dad's radio broadcasts when, there, in the corner opposite the radio, lodged in a nook, I saw a green bust, the death mask, of Dylan, exact duplicate of the one in at the centre in Swansea. How profoundly odd, how abrupt and bizarre, this totem. It hit me. All things considered.

Aeronwy led the last climb, one final rack of stairs to ascend, one more horizontal plane to transect.

Boat House: Upstairs Bedrooms

Outside the windows, shadows were gathering over the estuary as we hurried up and angled into the younger children's space. The immediate furnishings included a sizable doll's house.[5] She pointed to the small bed in the area "over there" as that of her younger brother Colm, and then, "This was my place, on this side, here." On the wall above her bed hung a poster with an image from the great American myth: huddling together, cowering on the side of the yellow-brick road are Scarecrow, Tin Man, Cowardly Lion, and Dorothy.

Aeronwy opened a door as she spoke, "And this was my Mum and Dad's room." I registered, above a tall chest of drawers, an iconic photograph, black-and-white, medium-long shot—ruddy, robust, windswept Caitlin and Dylan, side by side, sharing a jaunty angle into the wind. It might have been Worms Head, I thought. Beside it, a smaller square frame held a photograph of the extended-family, posed on some extended-family occasion.

As I lived and breathed, my mind accelerated: How on Earth could this be happening? How did life manage to place me here, precisely? Beside the bed of Caitlin and Dylan Thomas?

In a story about how the Welsh tell stories (in *A Daughter Remembers*), Aeronwy writes that "for most in Laugharne, time is a malleable abstraction, a mere follower, never a leader." Very well, fine. Suddenly, multiple time-frames became molten; stories and psychic impulses and convergences swirled round and round in my mind; too many and too much for my susceptible heart as twilight was fleeing over Afon Tâf.

I gazed up at the rafters, their mutely sentient matter. I felt that they were more infused than the other wood, glass, fabric. Rafters are generally less affected by the malleable abstractions of time. They are sentinels, above it all, absorbing it all. I too listened, did not lurk. I was not at all trying to lead my imaginings, but in my inner ears I felt the rumbling of soundless sounds. Empty echoes stoked my gray tissue. The very last time. That was all I could think about. I always think about last things. And I contemplated the last royal occasion they laid here as King and Queen, under these rafters. What was the character of that night in this contained space? What night?

The each of them and both of them, the mania, was too much for their containers. How did it come to pass, later, with the final cataclysm, that the dying supernova of their dreams erupted, and that radiation soaked into these beams? I couldn't help but wonder about the character of things, when it came to be that there was no way forward and no way back and no way anywhere. With the children a few whispers away. The whole superstructure was so small, all the interior cubes squeezed tightly against each other, on top of and below each other. His shed, his hut, was a few scant steps away, clinging to the cliff walk, toward town. He had finished it off, Buggerall. The town crier had gotten rotund.

There were westerly promises for him. Not more BBC work. The New World was breaking out Luftwaffe-free. He had a starring, virile role in his own mythos, and had an almost finished script. A larger than life life had sprung up beyond the sunset, riding with the gods where the rainbow ends. And no one but Dylan must play the part of Dylan. Cash venues. The 92nd Street Y coming on and coming on to overflowing. Frenetic enthusiasm. Fruition. A performing and recording artist he had become; his own label almost, almost his own genre; in America. Perhaps he could write again. Working plans with Stravinsky; a scenario for a libretto. Voluptuous epiphanies between the avenues. Trades of skin defying natural law. Poisons and potions. No barriers. Restlessness itself. Unsleeping around—the warm and dark blood mysteries come round again, the ring of dancing women and the fires within them.

They were all Caitlin, he said, in the end. If every male is in some way the son to every female in his life, then every such relationship is another opportunity for a Nogood Boyo-yo to fail. Seizure, outside-himself. Still yearning for the original, true, and everlasting Sublime. Religious. Oblation. Obliteration. Oblivion. He held high-voltage transmission lines with his bare hands in Lower Manhattan. He was willing to take his chances.

And she, in Laugharne? What about *she*? Her life story, her origins, her arising, her song and dance, all were as complicated as his, or more complicated. The daughter sometimes looks for the Big (and/or Great) Man for a father? Round and round and round it goes, and where it stops, nobody knows; it never stops. But after the last jig had been jigged, after the procreating had been accomplished, at that point in her life, what could she make happen on her own, without his powers of sun moon stars rain? She couldn't just put up with all the flying and going gallivanting? She couldn't come along with him, didn't want him to do America. Then, she did go along. Then he had some wild proposition, something like a residency at Stanford. California. She could catch up with him.[6]

Glorious wounds. No let up. As if they both had been bitten by the same venomous snake. Exactly how the geyser erupted under those rafters I could not and did not want to imagine. No details are necessary or desirable. Fusion, fission. Howls and screams. When they were both on the younger cusp of forty. About forty years for him, he had often said.

The Boat House was a provided place, for him to write in his shed, for her to keep together the household on the cliff. The Boat House was cold, damp, rodent-infested. Not a playhouse, not a fortress. She did not have what she had dreamed. "She'd had all this horrible life with him," as Miriam Patchen remembered her saying in San Francisco [Lycett]. Their life had become a nightmare. Cataclysmic domesticity. All dreams must change, and the bigger they are, the higher that cost might be. What remnants can one keep?

All houses must stand empty sometime. Maybe it is an abiding and universal emptiness that some people come to the Boat House to venerate.

Aeronwy called out that it was time to leave. Growing dim for the churchyard.

Interlude at Laugharne Castle

The light was falling fast on Dylan's Walk (so designated, I noted, on the street sign), as Aeronwy and I quickly passed the Writing Shed, into town, where, at the end of the path, Liz, Robin, and Peter were nowhere to be found. Peter had dropped us off, on our way in; thus, we had no clue where he had parked. Our lingering excursion had left us considerably behind. I checked driveways nearby. Futile.

We strode down to the wide square under the walls of Laugharne Castle, to the bottom end of town, sea level. At that moment, silhouetted against the twilight sky, the ruins were an elegant mass, securing the higher ground. I know I felt comforted—which is, after all, the point of a castle. I read about the stone circle and also the large hearthstone placed there a thousand years ago or more, prior to the castle walls.

But I was summoned out of the trance by our immediate predicament, losing light. Aeronwy wondered if the others had proceeded ahead of us to the churchyard, or perhaps to Browns Hotel or the Cross House Inn. There weren't too many other possibilities to consider, and she was in charge as we trod the streets and by-lanes. I suggested that she might call Peter on the cell phone. She did, but only got voicemail. We were not sure about the local reception. We had simply not accounted for the possibility of becoming separated.

We determined to walk to the churchyard. Not a problem for me. I was sufficiently enrapt. No worries. Aeronwy was more intent. As we were about to set off on foot, Eleri Rettalick, who had closed up the Boat House behind us, drove up. After she and Aeronwy discussed the situation, we jumped in Eleri's car and found the churchyard parking lot empty. Meanwhile, Aeronwy tried Peter, got voicemail again; tried texting. Frustration built.

"If worse comes to worse, we'll just take a train back to Swansea," she said.

"But I don't think they would have left without us," I responded, feeling how strange it was to be in an area not a quarter-mile square, and bereft—with all the benefits of cell phone, voicemail, texting, and transportation.

Eleri zipped us back to the castle parking lot and waited, idling. When another car appeared; I didn't recognize it in the dark, but it was they, who had wondered what had happened to us, thought we might have gone to the churchyard, circuited town and back, checked the watering places. Our two cars had probably passed in opposite directions twice.

I wondered how the whole episode might have appeared from the castle's crenellated turret, had some guard on the night shift, a few centuries ago, gazed down into the future, marveling how we could possibly come up with the technology.

The Gravesite

"Is it too late, too dark?" Aeronwy asked. Absolutely not. We drove, again, the short distance from the castle and pulled into the lot below St. Martin's Church. Aeronwy and Liz waited in the car while Peter, Robin, and I tread up the few stone steps to the right of the gray façade. A final few steps of packed mud wound to the right beneath a massive, wrenched trunk and thickly braided canopy of a tree. Yggdrasil, the World Tree, it appeared to be.

Walking a little farther across the spongy sod between plots with no particular distinctions, Peter suddenly stopped, stood, and called out, "There it is, there's the grave of Dylan Thomas."

We triangulated ourselves. I felt a wave of strange, intense relaxation. The vanishing daylight was fitting, complete. Peace. I felt peace surpassing understanding—his final destination. No further explanations needed. No disputations. In my cells, like stars, I sensed a vast pin-wheeling mandala centering on that sturdy white cross.

The small screen from the exhibit in Swansea, the black-and-white footage of the funeral images, the interment, paraded darkly in my mind, cross-referencing my immediate perceptions. I could correlate the cinematic carrying down of the casket; the jittery procession of heavy black coats; Caitlin with her blowing blond hair, in a walking swoon, held up by those on either side who were countering the pull of gravity.

Another superimposition. Another pull: the narratives of Dylan's dying days, the Chelsea Hotel, St. Vincent's Hospital. All at once the dusks of November 1953 and November 2008 were linked—syzygy. Fifty-five years, and dendritic aftershocks were still dissipating through the ground beneath my feet. The gates of hell, he said he had seen, and he said it more than once. Hour by hour. *Under Milk Wood* performed. The injections, the incursions, of who knows what Via Dolorosa, while the powers he had depended upon were blasting away his cell walls, his perennial battle-magic collapsing in cascades. Caitlin's emergency transoceanic rush. Gravitational tidal forces crashed in, crushing in his brain. The finality of the final hour. The casting of lots of lots. Casting the death mask.

All the headstones in St. Martin's churchyard are ranged downslope. All are heading back to the sea. Standing at the foot of the grave, facing the seaward flow, I read the Old English inscription on the cross:

In Memory of
Dylan Thomas
born Oct. 27 1914
died Nov. 9 1953
R.I.P.

He died within two weeks of his fortieth birthday, toward winter solstice, before the rebirth of the sun. I circumambulated down beside Peter and read on the reverse side:

In Memory of
Caitlin Thomas
born Dec. 8 1913
died Aug. 1 1994
R.I.P.

Forty-one years after him, by her choice, Caitlin's body was interred there.

Peter said, "Caitlin is buried on top."

Lux Æterna

Day was dashed totally into night, but the impression of that bright white cross, burned in my retinas, faded slowly. To be sure, that cross in that cemetery is a center, a still point. Countless takes have been taken, are taken, will be taken. Pilgrimage. And so much written and said, about him, them, their lives, their early and later deaths. Sooner and later, we are all going that way. He took his own takes, continuously, and wrote them down from a very early age. He speaks very well and thoroughly on his own behalf. In the *Collected Poems*, dedicated *To Caitlin*, he has placed these words in the prologue, for us, his "readers, the strangers":

> *These poems, with all their crudities, doubts, and confusions, are written for the love of Man and in praise of God, and I'd be a damn' fool if they weren't.*

Amen, and amen.

Life came at them fast. The whole world was berserk, spinning out of control. They kept moving, to overwhelm the odds. Sometimes he crawled on all fours, reeling, intolerably drunk, letting his feelings function, proclaiming what he already had, and had lost, and could never have.

Bewildered, ensnared, seduced, deluded, betraying, betrayed, duped by self as much as by others, dismembered, disintegrating. None of these fates particularly distinguish one epitaph from the next.

But what is brought up, brought down, rendered, surrendered, brought out—there is the love. Behold that.

He didn't march off to war, no. They also serve, now and then, who only lie down and implode. He broke his very self down to the very particles, a sacrifice he freely accepted, and picked himself up again, over and over and over. A good son of Wales, doing what he could do. He suited up, showed up, and showed off, to the max, as often as possible.

The rage, the rave, transformed, becomes light. Not gentle, that blast of rays.

That does not die.

Browns Hotel

Aeronwy was still in the lead. We drove down from St. Martin's, a few short blocks back into town, to the Cross House Inn, to share a table, time free, in that native realm. Aeronwy bears with completeness her situation as daughter of the great man and woman. The circle is unbroken. Cross House is a family place, Welsh style. Loud music and laughter.

The keeper of the tavern informed Aeronwy that Browns Hotel was lit for the evening. That historic place, bought, sold, offered, unbought, is in limbo, a disturbance in the force. So it was a synchronicity that the doors would be open to us. We paced ourselves across the square to the two-story frontage with large plain letters over the entrance: BROWNS HOTEL.

In the hallway, well kept as it remains not too well kept, hang photographs of Dylan and Caitlin and company in various poses—a little showbiz. He, she, and both frequented Browns, as if the solutions, in any given hour, to the whole plunging world, could be found at a bar, a hotel. A distinct cultural legacy is visible at Browns. It, too, is a shrine.

We turned to a small, triple-iron-legged tavern table set in a window cove next to the street. On the wall, a photograph of the smiling Caitlin and smiling Dylan, in their prime, in the fullness of their time, in the exact same spot, unaltered to this very day. We situated ourselves, Aeronwy in the middle, and took it all in. Opposite us, across the small room, the bar was populated by smart youth. As if the bar were the stage and we were the audience. Or, just as much, the table where we sat was the stage, and they were our audience. I was aware of a knowing glance now and then toward Aeronwy, in her position.

All I could think of was the younger Caitlin, dancing on tabletops, and the later Dylan—bard, broadcaster, American sensation—in tweeds. Booze and cigarettes. Browns was more hospitable than the Boat House. Did those two know how to live, or what?

It was to Browns that the funeral party adjourned from St. Martin's in 1953. Caitlin was in no condition to hear that he had left her, intestate, with £100, and the literary properties. Voices buzzing around her.

Across the street stands The Pelican, the residence for Dylan's parents through his father's final years. Florrie lived afterward in the Boat House after Dylan too had died and after Caitlin left permanently for Elba.

We didn't have drinks at Browns but drove back to Swansea and on to Mumbles, had dinner, bid farewell to Aeronwy, who was catching a train back to London early the next morning. Robin and Liz proceeded upstairs. I split with Peter the sandwiches from the Boat House. They made my breakfast for the next couple of days.

No. 5 Cwmdonkin Drive

Next morning, Peter whisked us out of the hotel and uphill via Cwmdonkin Drive. The name [Koom-donk-in] is Welsh for "donkey common." We parked on the street, and stepped out to a sweeping vista of Swansea, the shoreline, the horizon. A dropped tennis ball might, theoretically, bounce all the way down to Oystermouth Road and onto the beach. We ambled up the sidewalk to the corner, to No. 5. It is a plain but solid, two-story, Edwardian-ish duplex. The first-story exterior is gray plaster; second story is shingled wood. Streetside, two-story bay windows protrude. The front entrance jogs off to the right of the façade.

Nothing remarkable, I thought, as Peter walked up to the door. I caught sight of a large, blue, ceramic medallion, prominent at the corner of the house next to the entrance, stating in large white script:

DYLAN THOMAS
A man of words
1914 – 1953
was born in
this house

In the doorway, we posed for pictures.

D. J. and Florrie Thomas had consolidated their standing in the community when they moved into their new house. It was on a corner lot, in a freshly developed residential area, in the Uplands, opposite the industrial and working class side of Swansea. Peter pointed to the bay window of the special bedroom, guest room, where Dylan was born two months after the onslaught of the Great War.

The house has been carefully restored, outside and in, is now let out for a few nights at a time, as Peter informed us. We did not have an appointment to go inside, and no one was there, but my mental images of the floorplan were clear enough from my studies; the rooms of Nancy and her younger brother, their parents' room. I imagined a sturdy gas range where Florrie warmed milk for making milquetoast, the semi-liquid meal that her son loved most. And of course, inside is the study where D. J. escaped to mark papers and make sense. And naturally there lay the parlour.

We stepped away from the entrance and walked out to the street corner and along the flank of the house to survey the backyard and Dylan's bedroom window. That bedroom was his for more than half his life, including, as he termed it, an "incurable adolescence" when he had extended periods alone with himself. He had produced "The force that through the green fuse," "Death has no dominion," and two-thirds of his Poetic Output before he was twenty.

He took to referring to himself as "the Rimbaud of Cwmdonkin Drive." And what clues are there? Nothing visible. Or anything and everything, obviously. *In toto.*

Cwmdonkin Park

Peter led us the short distance from No. 5 to Cwmdonkin Park. Blackbirds sang among the rustling leaves. Magpies chattered above thick moss and hard-packed mud paths. Ferns splayed over exposed roots, heavily entwined. We walked the same route that Florrie walked with her special boy, her luminous boy, the invested son of Wales, squealing vowel sounds. By 1916, the toddler would have been offering a few intelligible words. Hopping and skipping along with his sister Nancy, he would have been shaping whole sentences and questions under the forest canopy by 1919—year of the pandemic flu and death on a scale not seen since the Plague.

We followed down and around to the spot where stood luminous the exact cast-iron *fountain basin,* as he put it ("Hunchback in the park"), *where I sailed my ship.* It has the look of a baptismal, alchymic font. Still a murmuring fountain it is, with a silver pool large enough to see your face in.

He emphasized the power of this green-gold Eden. I could perceive the primacy of its perceptual unfolding and

enfolding, deep and warm—the spell rising up from
below.

Winding downhill and around, we came upon a
memorial slab laid low in a brace of vines. Placed in 1963
by Holdridge and Roney of Caedmon Records, it was for
some time the only commemoration of Dylan in his
hometown, Peter noted. In the surface are chiseled the
lines:

> Oh as I was young and easy in the mercy of
>   his means,
> Time held me green and dying
> Though I sang in my chains like the sea.

If it's hell to be expelled from the Garden, it is death to
be held back, contained. The park is a kept space, granted
reprieve, allowed, maintained. It was, of course, not
enough. Swansea was not enough. Laugharne. London.
Oxford. All. Not enough, betwixt the devil and the deep
blue sea.

Into the Labyrinth, Swansea

We reversed our path, trod back uphill. A young mother, cell phone to ear, bright-eyed child in stroller, pushed vigorously past us. Snapping our seatbelts, we drove through the Uplands, fully built out with multi-story condos rising to skyline views of Swansea and bay.

Very close by, Peter directed our attention to the stone walls of Mirador Crescent Nursery School. He drove around the block to give us all a second chance to pick out the structure where the younger Dylan shaped his letters, stacked blocks, and even declaimed poetry. Suburbia it was then, a neighborhood of substance, and much more so now, no doubt.

The Swansea that Dylan grew up in had been destroyed by incendiary bombs, targeted by Hitler's directive to blast away British seaports. Rebuilding took decades, and it is a commonplace sensibility, according to Peter, that whatever the air raids didn't destroy or disfigure, poor urban planning did. I noticed that not too many people seem actually to live toward the center of the city; they're mostly somewhere else, in mostly undisclosed locations. But in whatever ways it's all coming together and not, sustaining itself and not, downtown Swansea felt a little jumbled and out-of-focus and (not sentimentally, no, no) endearing to me.

We drove through the area where stood the original Swansea Grammar School, now with a different name. There D. J. Thomas was Senior English Master, and there Dylan attended, without distinctions, age ten to age sixteen—the extent of his formal education. The books at Cwmdonkin Drive, the treasury of his father's literary quest, had been more influential. D. J. read Shakespeare and Keats aloud to Dylan as a child. Also, D. J. was a great fan of Thomas Hardy, so those tomes would have been on the study shelves. Virtually all the seminal works of English literature were there to be found. D. H. Lawrence was surely available to Dylan as he began to explore his own *logoi spermatakoi*. As to Swansea Grammar School, after 1941, only fragments of the original structures remained. Much of the 18th century building had been gutted by incendiary bombs.

As we entered the zone of Swansea Metropolitan University, the street demographics changed. Fine arts, design, media, architectural glass, and the stained glass windows the university is known for, Peter explained. Lots of vivacious undergrads, I noticed, were plying the storefronts between collegiate flats. I wondered about them, and how it is for them, coming of age in Swansea, almost a decade deep in the 21st century.

Toward the town center, we passed the Palace Theatre, a structural survivor of the bombing. It had been a music hall for Charlie Chaplin, and later, Sir Anthony Hopkins first took the professional stage there. I saw crowds spilling out of an adjacent watering spot, numerous bobbies patrolling. A football crowd, I suspected.

We passed the *Swansea Evening News* building, a multi-story rectangular block of aluminum and glass. I thought of Dylan's work for the *South Wales Daily Post*, and the sense of reportage that he gained there as he expanded his perceptions beyond Cwmdonkin.

Peter suddenly swerved to the side and stopped in front of a classic brick building. "This is the BBC, where Dylan made some of his broadcasts." Dylan had first performed on the air at age 22, in 1937, only ten years after the BBC itself had been founded. I peered intently.

We wound near the Tawe riverfront to the Marina that has replaced the old South Dock. I recognized that we had returned to the vicinity of the Dylan Thomas Centre, another structure that escaped the wrath of the bombs. Residual vibrations of the old industrial area, the old working port, the early 18th century, registered in my bones. After all, Wales was the very cradle of industrialization the first nation in the world to have a higher proportion of its workforce employed in industry than in agriculture, as I read on a web search. That threshold was, in fact, attained in 1851. Think King Copper. Anthracite. Welsh miners, the iconic images.

We parked near the Sail Bridge, ultra-modern, a pedestrian bridge, and walked to the square formed on one side by the National Waterfront Museum. Behind a wide window is an original two-story tram car of the Swansea and Mumbles Railway — the kind of car Dylan rode to his theatrical rehearsals and conjunctions in Oystermouth.

In one quadrant of the square, off-center, is a life-size, seated bronze of Dylan. Peter said, "I don't think it really captures him, but it is better than no statue at all." Beyond it stands a bronze Captain Kat, a character from *Under Milk*

Wood. Much ado about Dylan. Dylan upon Dylan, after Dylan. Dylan approximately. I wasn't sure if I were finding him or losing him.

We filed along through a Saturday morning crafts fair and into a cafeteria line, made lunch selections, found a table. Large-format photographs, good work, hung from the high ceiling for context; with rich displays of stained glass.

Peter had papers to mark, gave us a lift to the hotel. For the rest of the afternoon I was free as a breeze.

Lavender Dusk, Abertawe

A return trip all the way to Worms Head for a final meal together was the plan for later. Meanwhile, I took my laptop to the lobby, checked email, and set off for the city centre. I edged past the Marina condos and recent construction, edging the perimeter of the old quay made of huge, rough-hewn stone blocks. Quarried by Druids, you could convince me. I rounded a corner toward the vicinity of Swansea Castle and was surprised to find myself smack in front of the Swansea Museum with its slate gray façade. We had driven past it earlier, "a museum that belongs in a museum," quoth Dylan, according to Peter, adding that it is essentially unchanged since Dylan's time. Sensational! I stepped inside. Besides the docents fully engaged in their huddle at the entrance, I had the whole place to myself.

Cases of fossils, Stone Age fragments, artifacts. More bliss. A shard of a square ceramic serving plate was stamped AUGUSTUS, an artifact from the soldiers' barracks of the Roman occupation. The magnificent displays of medieval collections included intricately carved wood and hammered metal objects of every description, grails of Arthurian-Merlinian character. Essentially *in situ*, I felt.

Nearing closing time, I leaped to the Industrial Revolution, the era of King Copper, iron, coal. But then, then, my favorite chamber opened up. It was sort of an ultimate Welsh parlour, overflowing with Georgian, Victorian, Edwardian antiques—priceless rummage in the community attic.

And then, beyond its own ante-chamber, unsealed, dis-encased, I found myself completely alone and face to face with an authentic Egyptian mummy. What an exotic mirroring. The mummy both disclosed and concealed its significations and mysteries, as curated in Victorian Swansea at the height of the British Empire. The exhibit exhibits the assumptions of its exhibiting. Dylan nailed it. There was unfinished business there, spanning several millennia. But not for me to resolve.

Closing time. I hurried downstairs, a docent locking the doors behind me.

Onward, downtown. Turning the corner of every block I seemed to find a new ambiance not overtly connected to what I'd just left behind. Night life venues were starting to kindle while comparison shoppers were wrapping up their afternoon. Oxford Street. Princess Street. The New York Pub. The vertical, red brick mass of St. David's Shopping Centre (named for the national saint) seemed, through street-level windows, mostly defunct, except for multiplex cinema. Multi-story parking structures here and there. Bus station. No-Sign Bar. Office accommodations. A gay bar; didn't catch the name. Wind Street (a Dylan haunt). Salubrious Place, a covered alleyway, was strangely vacant between everyone's leaving and anyone's arriving.

I had found myself on a tangent with St. Mary's Church a couple of times, so I decided to check it out. The original church was built in 1328, as I read in the nave. Nave roof collapsed in 1739 with congregation barely making it outside; 1822, gas lit; 1896, everything flattened for rebuilding; extensively destroyed by bombs, 1941; 1950s rebuilt. A youth choir was in rehearsal when I stepped in. I got the feeling of a true commons. Not sedate. No pretensions. I liked St. Mary's.

Back outside, I crossed over to Swansea Market, an enclosed mall with Welsh flavorings. Those my age were a distinct minority, I discerned, among the waves of young men and nubile young women, shopping and otherwise. I was also aware, by comparison with any given US setting, of a lack of diversity. Statistically, not many of these young people or their parents were born outside the UK; those who are non-native-Welsh have mostly in-migrated from England. And another thing, while all the signs showed the Welsh names, I never heard the language spoken anywhere. Welsh, to the casual pilgrim, is a visual and not an auditory experience.

Teen spirit mounted through the Musiquarium with its racks of CDs and DVDs. Suddenly, the poetry of Dylan Thomas—poetry in general—seemed rather small in imaginal scale. How are Dylan's poems faring with the Swansea Market crowd? I wondered if it would matter to communicate that it was from Dylan, I'd say, that James Dean learned how to place a cigarette on his lip? I said, James Dean. I wondered how, in *The Edge of Love,* the lives of Dylan and Caitlin would be cinemaestheticized in Blu-Ray. Powerful forces, the *Zeitcapital* and so forth, that through the attention-economy drive the archetypal images.

I stumbled fast-forward into the twilight, toward the seated bronze Dylan, aiming for the hotel.

November brings the Winter Festival to the square adjacent to the Leisure Center, a municipal sports and conditioning facility. Carnival rides, attractions for kids of all ages, sideshows, all were available, enticing. An ice-skating rink had quite a few skaters gliding along. There was a respectable Ferris Wheel. I had spied it on arrival in Swansea, and I had a little more time. I bought some tokens. Shortly, the wheel stopped. I was directed to my own pod, an enclosed cage; snapped shut. I was all settled when the operator wickedly spun my pod. I love Ferris Wheel motion, and roller coaster motion; I hate centrifugal motion. I did my best to resist. Then the wheel began to roll. Only one other pod was occupied, by a father and a toddler who screamed and screamed. After one revolution, the wheel stopped; father and toddler disembarked. I was the only rider left. Once again, off, the wicked spin, and up I went. And down, again.

The western sky was turning lavender. With each ascending arc, I took in the celestial waters. And with each descent, I took in the terrestrial scene of Abertawe — "mouth of the Tawe" — as Swansea is known by its Welsh name.

With equal stresses: Aber-ta-weh (as in wet).

Gwyr

All into the car with Peter, driving west again. He pointed out, "Catherine Zeta-Jones resided there a while," and, "That's the way to the Burton home," where lived Philip Burton, the adoptive father of Richard Burton. We passed the campus of the University of Wales. All together, there must be a substantial collegiate population in the city and county of Swansea.

Out of Swansea, we again swerved through the ravines, wilds, fields, meadows, silences, and intrigues of Gower—*Gwyr*. The Welsh name means "bent, crooked." In preparation for this return trip, I had done some web research and learned that the earliest known human fragment discovered in Cymru is the tooth of an individual who lived and died 230,000 years ago, Paleolithic times. Also, early in the 19th century, a complete human skeleton, dyed in red ochre, was found in a limestone cave in Gwyr; a young male who lived 29,000 years ago; a ceremonial burial, with ivory and seashell jewelry, the skull of a mammoth. It is the oldest known burial in Western Europe.

As Peter negotiated the bends in the road, I re-negotiated my thoughts of human experience in this terrain in the course of 230 millennia. Not that long in terms of continental drift, no. But that young male buried here only twenty-nine millennia ago lived in a community that was dealing with the last climax of glaciation. That was prior to the domestication of cattle, or dogs, or cats. That westerly-most European burial was accomplished 5,000 years before the Venus of Willendorf was carved; 13,000 years before painters carried their polychrome crayons into the cavernous depths at Altamira and Lascaux. Even the standing stones—menhirs—that I knew to be, but did not see, standing in Gwyr, are a little more recent. (If I journey to Wales again, I must search out a menhir, cromlech, a holy well.)

Epochs ebbed and flowed in my imaginings as we drove. Bronze Age, Iron Age. All societies arising in their seasons. Raids, conquests, revolts without ceasing. Roman attacks against the Silurian and Ordovician tribes, their slow subjugation to Roman laws, the creation of Roman roads, forts, mines. The medieval kingdoms. Welsh bards, harps, heavenly instruments. Celts, Angles, Saxons, Vikings, Normans. Arthur, Merlin. Conversions, Christian churches built on top of Celtic stone circles. Here. There. Close. All connected. Connecting.

Past Rhossili, we parked once more in the lot beside the tavern at the inn, at the end. Too dark and windy this time to peer over the cliffs to the beach. Too cold. But it could have been this spot where Dylan and Caitlin posed, glamorously disheveled, for the photograph that hangs above the dresser in the Boat House. Moving inside, warmed by the fire, we had a good long conversation over a couple of rounds.

We talked about Dylan's art and sullen craft. And Caitlin. The sexual vectors. The word magic, the love magic. What they fought for. What is stored up in the lore and in the body of his work. The labors, the distillations. The stone in the wind.

We polished off our last dinner. Solid, Welsh, complete. We were outside and ready to go when we spotted the sharp horns of the crescent moon. Older than old, newer than new. Piercing the last impulse of the northwestern glow.

Night Codes, Trawler Road

The code of night tapped on my tongue
—Dylan Thomas,
"From love's first fever to her plague"

I am incapable of more knowledge.
—Sylvia Plath

The sacrifices of God are a broken spirit.
—Psalm 51

Back at the hotel, with the window open to the beach and the wind, I packed, did some reading about Dylan, the "schizoid diagnosis"—that Humpty-Dumpty had fallen off the wall at a very young age. The crack could have occurred between nursery and grammar school. Or even earlier; from the get-go, perhaps, there were doubts among the infantile fissures and grievances about himself. A child in the Great War. There were few precedents in human experience for such a context and situation as the Battle of the Somme, as it occurred when he breathed his first lexical sounds and syllables in the family's brand new dream house on Cwmdonkin Drive.

He was the original rebel without a cause, in this reading. Something immediately abstract, too unreal to be spoken of, but too real to be denied, and still it was denied as much as it was recognized, and it affected everything. The lad somehow had access to too much truth. He was peculiarly sensitive to and able to communicate in codes certain secret strata of society. But he was never too good with money, train tickets, or a clean shirt. Something was always awry. But he mostly managed his appointed rounds, sometimes with extraordinary adeptness and an abiding sense of duty. In a disintegrating world, self-destruction can be an honorable or at least necessary form of self-control. Psychic survival can be pursued, and at times must be pursued, by means of regression. He was willing not to make sense of what was nonsensical, 1914–1953, and still to speak, thoughtfully, gratefully, and very powerfully.

And what else is the patient saying? An acute and particular yearning for heart connection, I'd say. The original and archaic and universal need for unconditional love, acceptance, couldn't be more loud and clear, by my reading. What powerful efforts by the Welsh poet have been made. Did he not take on full-force his service-sector job?

All packed, teeth brushed. I stood by the window, breathed in the cold, and then crawled in, yanked my blanket tight. No run next morning; Peter was to be downstairs very early.

Great Circles

Cardiff, Amsterdam, Minneapolis, San Francisco. CWL to AMS to MSP to SFO. I was up well before sunrise and down to the lobby, wi-fi. Hello to the overnight desk clerk. Checking my flights, Mumbai images unrelenting on the flat screen; no break in the siege. Upstairs to finish off the last couple of sandwiches from Laugharne. Back down to the lobby with my bag. Checkout. Peter walked through the door. We were off to the M4 in the Monday morning traffic to Cardiff. It was difficult to say anything more about Dylan or Cymru without coffee. At the airport, Peter dropped me off, goodbyes at the curb, and he circled back to meet his class on time.

Inside too soon to check my bag, I found a corridor to myself. As I watched the airport staff park, lock their cars, and amble in, a slight pink hue appeared in the east over the beautiful Vale of Glamorgan. That was good enough for me, and I devoted myself to early Dawn Arising. Eventually I checked in, made it through security, enjoyed a facsimile of a traditional Welsh breakfast in a broad section of empty tables. Boarded my flight in due course.

In flight to Amsterdam, a stunning celestial event had begun—a conjunction of Venus and the Moon with Jupiter in proximal triangulation. A sign in the heavens. I enjoyed that changing trigonometry in flight all the way around the Earth.

Glancing out at 39,000 feet, I tried to relax my body. Again, I could not control obsessing about atmospheric turbidity. Dozing in and out, through the duration of the flight, I gazed down for a while on the perishing ice of Greenland. Then came the frozen islands of Newfoundland. And finally I was able to relax, south of Hudson Bay, on our long slow glide path into Minneapolis. A pleasant layover in the North Country fair, and then one more arc carried me to the Pacific and ground transpo to Monterey and to Carmel, west of the west of things, as Jeffers puts it.

So much of Wales and of the powers of Dylan's incantations to metabolize—I am changed by all that is terribly unresolved. And un-resolvable.

Shaken by all of this.

EPILOGUE

Beyond The Horizon

The prominent poems, a few stories, a few vinyl LPs that I used in my teaching. That is what I had known of Dylan Thomas. Questions I carried to Wales: What is the work I have to do here? Where might the work lead? I had zero expectation of writing, or of being able to write, anything about the experience. I took zero notes. But the story emerged on its own. When I had finished sending my journal segments, plain email texts, to a few readers around the world, my friend Ty Griffin suggested that my working title, *Finding Dylan Thomas in the 21st Century*, was not the title I had intended but rather the subtitle for the main one that I had yet to find.

I turned to the last pages of the *Collected Poems* and scanned "In the white giant's thigh," among Dylan's last and most complex poems. Among the closing stanzas I found:

> *. . . to these*
> *Hale dead and deathless do the women of the hill*
> *Love for ever meridian through the courters' trees*

I put on the CD, from the box set my friend Carolyn Kleefeld had given me, and listened to Dylan read those lines again and again. I felt an opening through them, a portal. The key stuck in my mind, regarding the *Hale dead and deathless . . . Love for ever meridian.*

As I walk through this opening, holding this key, I am grateful for having gotten to know more deeply his life and love among the ruins of the first half of the 20th century. I have read how many persons were drawn to him throughout his lifetime, persons who not only cared about him, but who also wanted to take care of him, to his dying day. I have come to the conclusion that at the core he was an intensely loving person. No sentimentality here (un-Welsh? un-British?), but he wanted to love and to be loved. He said so. He was a boy and a man, never an old man, who wanted to be wanted. That's human enough.

I wondered, among the dead and deathless, how "loving" might be "for ever meridian." I looked up the etymology: **meridian** > *meridianus,* of noon. *Medius + die,* the middle of the day, from an Indo-European root meaning "bright sky," extended from *di-, deya-, dei-,* to shine, glitter; as with "deity." Thus, meridian, the everyday relation of the Sun and the rotating Earth. And divine, why not? Behold, the Cosmic Wheel.

Of course, who knows the *poeisis* in Dylan's mind when this phrase irrupted? Perhaps it was simply that along with "ante"-meridian loving (in the a.m.) and the "post"-meridian loving (in the p.m.), we have also "for ever"-meridian loving at any time and all the time, shining, glittering.

That's a couple of takes, anyway.

Love for-e-ver mer-i-di-an has the same cadence as Death shall have no do-min-i-on.

How do the Symbols manifest in strange and eerie directness, signaling the wider dimensions of infancy and childhood, adolescence incurable or otherwise, ripeness, and that final good night, obliteration?

He was always circumambulating, twisting turning through the tensions, this way, that way, as they appeared and disappeared, the huntsman out and about. Then he sought his way back to house, hearth, table, bed—to Her, to Life. It is Life we turn toward, we turn away from; we emerge and spiral forth. Magic, myth. Rationalizations. Our lives configure, de-configure, re-configure, in realizations and unrealizations. *Complexio oppositorum.* In his stories, in all our stories.

I am always looking for some Rock at the center. And what I look for, I find: the rock of Cwmdonkin above the bay that slopes for ever. The Precambrian rock of Gwyr laid down over a half-billion years ago. I think of the young male buried in that rock 29,000 years ago, while I obsess about how we humans are going to manage our planetary responsibilities for the next hundred-thousand years and more, and for ever. How do we humans even recognize ourselves for who we truly are? One way is to follow the path past the stone circle, the hearth at Laugharne Castle, to the escarpment with the Writing Shed on stilts, to the Boat House shrine. We can take a walking tour where the Chelsea Hotel and St. Vincent's Hospital rest on billion year old Manhattan gneiss. We can locate the rock, laid down, volcanic-arc, of origin, at the center. Blessed be.

In this creative process, then, concentrate the Prima Materia—with enormous heat and pressure—until diamonds form, or else the Magnum Opus disintegrates; in one life, it is possible that both may happen. Pray, love, love again. Radical love is not less powerful in its catastrophes. Radical love sometimes means flying apart, losing it. The sacrifice. Holy love is alive in its earthiest mutations. The hidden/not-so-hidden power of the archaic rage, the rant of arising, is too much for any one of us to contain, or for any community that any of us is born into and carry inside of us, recognized or not, to contain. The sky is filled with diamonds.

Venturing through the labyrinth always has to do with our life-and-death situation, as Dylan, it seems, was born knowing. A labyrinth, traditionally, is located in a cave. For a poet, generally, the cave is a self. Passages include the Land of the Dead, decisions that must be made in the underworld, and judgments that only there can be obtained. The presiding personage is always a woman, the Muse, or otherwise. The labyrinth must be walked or danced through, for rebirth, life after death—initiation.

After this journey, re-enacting something of his trajectories, after this writing, I want my back and neck muscles to relax. I am ready for the tension around my eyes to let go. I'd like the tensional pattern in my forehead to release. I'm feeling a little unsteady. The problem is not just in my mind. It is in my brain, the gelatinous mass of this physical organ over here. The dis-ease is in my guts, the coils of my entrails, as I circle this menhir, as I have crawled back and down inside this dolmen, curling into fetal position, recycling through these fields and particles. Primal fear forms in compressions of gravity, a giant's thigh, a graveyard. I feel my blood pressure dizzily as I hold the planetary emergency—the larger story—deep in my body cavity.

Following the ghost of Mr. Dylan Thomas, falling into nothingness, I am wrenched from the inside out. Of course, how a pilgrimage leads the pilgrims along, one by one, is what it is all about. How doth the Symbols manifest themselves? Appearances, apparitions. Illuminated mists. Assorted clews. The Dionysiac, the Picaresque. Presto-chango. The jokes. Bravado. Emblems. Abysses, whirlpools beneath castle walls. Purgatories. Surrounded by the orbits of celestial bodies, immersed in the Milky Way. Braneworlds in fractals enfold deeper and further in the divine inscrutability. Extinctions, vanishings. With the planet over and overheating faster and faster, I reach the final stage of my projections to find the poet apocalyptical: Dylan, son of a sea wave, drowning in his own flames.

How is it any given individual comes to consciousness? How does a particular genius come to be? A lightning bolt, a ground charge, rises up out of the Earth, stroke and return-stroke. Among other ways, Dylan described himself as "sin-eater." What created him and destroyed him, restores him. He participated as fully as he could—*for the love of Man and in praise of God, and I'd be a damn' fool*, he said, *to do otherwise.*

I have here at hand an oyster shell, densely built, its surface wildly and weirdly ruffled like a crinoline—as I spotted it last November, seathumbed, and shining forth in the wet sand on Swansea Beach.

Waking up one more time. That's it. Alleluia. Pilgrimage indeed.

April 2009

New York City, June 1, 2009

The Hotel Chelsea is haunted, all right. To that I can testify, as I now lean back on this daybed set in an alcove. These south-facing windows are wide open, for the early summer breezes off the Hudson, the street smells, for the after-midnight sounds of 7th/8th Avenues—relatively quiet in early Monday morning hours—all rising up these seven stories.

Yes, I have felt anomalies in the psychic field here.

First off, I located the door of Room 206, the last door Dylan Thomas walked through. Nearby is Room 211, where Bob Dylan wrote "Sad-Eyed Lady of the Lowlands," and most of *Blonde on Blonde.*

Then, I took the stairs to the tenth floor and stood before the door, painted silver-metallic, where Arthur C. Clark "checked into my new suite, 1008," on July 1, 1964— almost a half-century ago. Through that door, Stanley Kubrick, having finished *Dr. Strangelove,* arrived so that the two of them could get to work on *2001: A Space Odyssey.*[7]

And with all the other lore as well, I have found the Chelsea to be multi-dimensionally welcoming.[8] Shining.

Peter Thabit Jones is here in the city, along with those of us who hosted Aeronwy and him in 2008, convened by Stan Barkan.[9] We've had readings at the New York Public Library and at Baruch College. Yesterday, Peter led the Dylan Thomas Walking Tour of Greenwich Village, by the scheme that he and Aeronwy created.[10]

Yesterday, our tour began at the Church of St. Luke-in-the-Fields, where the memorial service for Dylan was held just before Caitlin departed with his body, re-crossing the Atlantic on the *United States*. In my college years, late 60s–early 70s, I hung out in that neighborhood with my friend Peter Ainslie, in his place on Grove Street. I had barely registered the old church then, at the end of Grove, on Hudson. I was unaware that it was the third church erected on the island of Mannahatta, built when the Village zone was open, rolling countryside—not all that long ago.

I arrived at St. Luke's early to join the Pentecost liturgy in progress. I stood at the back among the alleluias and breathed the clouds of incense. Baptisms were set for bright-eyed babies born nearly a decade deep in the 21st century.

Our entourage formed in the rose garden at noon, and after invocations and formalities, we set out following Peter. We walked past the site of Chumley's, the bar long defunct. Next, we trekked past Minetta's Tavern. Minetta was the Indian name for the stream that, though buried, still runs. We meandered around The Cherry Lane Theater, established by Edna St. Vincent Millay. Dylan read there in 1953. We had drinks in a bar that was once the literary San Remo. We sauntered past the Café Wha? at the corner of Bleecker and McDougal. In the shady, flowered courtyard at Patchin Place, we congregated in front of the apartment where E. E. Cummings and Marion Morehouse lived for forty years, until he died. E. E. was a champion of Dylan.

As the shadows lengthened, we found the old main entrance of St. Vincent's Hospital on 10th. The light was golden tangible, full of promise on the last day of May. I imagined the final hours of Dylan's life, enclosed behind those red brick walls, and how the light might have played that November.

Our final destination was the legendary White Horse, The Horse, Dylan's favorite. It has landmark status as the locus of his final tavern experience. The lore centers on his famous last words: "I've just had eighteen whiskies, I think that's a record." In truth, the bartender that night said he had only about six whiskies. There is a plaque on a wall somewhere; I didn't see. Others report that Dylan later had a few more words to say anyway.

After lounging at the White Horse for a while, we Village pilgrims dispersed. I had a little more time to talk things over with Peter, on Dylan's poetry, timeless as it is, and how the body of his work does not yield to superficial readings. "In the white giant's thigh," I mentioned—that convolute, eerie, mystic, demanding, late poem. True bard he was, and poet-martyr, I suggested, however that happens. Peter and I discussed the idiosyncrasies, the paradoxes, the grand un-reliabilities *in flagrante delicto...* And, *how might students in this not-so-new century find him?* An open question.

Bidding Peter farewell, I left the back room and headed toward the venerable bar where Dylan had often stood, smack dab at the middle of things, at the center of attention, spinning about, in the bosom of his new world. At the corner of that bar, Dylan performed his dazzling improv—cadenced, no doubt—and stand-up comedy, the flamboyant impersonations of his own bardic self/non-self. No automatic badge of honor in the post-War Village just for showing up Welsh. He had to entertain to survive, to engage. Belonging is more important than being understood, or even approved of. Wild belonging it was. The Horse.

Hanging on the wall at the far end of the bar—I spotted it—was the framed photograph (by Bunny Adler) of Dylan himself, standing at the corner of the bar where I was, in fact, myself standing. *Abracadabra!* In the photograph, taken from the perspective over my shoulders, Dylan is shown with his right hand grasping a mug, a cigarette between the fingers of his left hand, his tweed coat buttoned and strained tightly around his chest and belly. His face is blazing—three sheets to the wind, and far, far from it. It is supernal, that glazed-over look in his face. *Behold the Man.*

Then, as I wheeled around for a parting glance, my eyes caught a very large canvas. With shades of gray acrylics, a painter has reproduced, enlarged, interpreted, and expanded upon Bunny Adler's photograph, accentuating and intensifying the look in Dylan's eyes, light-rays striking out. What I see through those eyes is battle fatigue, shell shock, the Past passing like a cataclysmic electrical storm off the Atlantic—and new horizons in the West, of a Future exploding, thermonuclear shockwaves ringing a mushroom cloud. Suddenly, I find myself standing with him in this hall of mirrors, fractal, kaleidoscopic.

I could not just stand there *for ever.* I stepped out the door at the corner of Hudson and 11th and breathed. Then I trod along. I rambled around the twists and turns I knew forty-plus years ago, all the street names chiming like cathedral bells. In the fullness of time, I caught the subway back here to my miraculous little kitchenette, to make a salad, have a beer, lay my body down.

As we all shine on.

Manhattan is not a large island by area, but it has indeed become a thoroughly occupied island in the four centuries since Henry Hudson sailed up the west side in 1609. Wolves roamed in the area now called Washington Heights when the manor house at Fern Hill was built in 1723.[11] Things have always moved fast here; that's no news. The pace of change is accelerating everywhere — Dylan Thomas's 100th birthday coming soon. Dylan's centennial will also be the centennial of the start of the War to End All Wars. How are those dead going to be remembered among the living? Dylan's own incantations are vaster than the understandings he never pretended to achieve. What he found, he offered with all his heart.

Earlier tonight on this daybed, I watched Kubrick's first feature film: *Killer's Kiss*, the great noir film set in a New York. I watched *Space Odyssey* for the nth time, visualizing the effects of the Chelsea environs on Kubrick and Clark's creative process. I reviewed several scenes of *Eyes Wide Shut*, Kubrick's last film, also set in NYC. I watched these three films beside these open windows, as the moon rose over SoHo. The "capital of the world" is how the young Bob Dylan thought about it, when he first showed up here, when he felt his call "to reach the world."[12]

We all shine on, as the city contemplates itself. The city is us. So what is it we human beings are becoming as we imagine together, like it our not, our global realities? What does an artist do? Peter and I talked about Dylan's last dreams, his project with Stravinsky—the libretto he was developing about survivors of nuclear war, something of Dr. Strangelove in operatic form.

Eyes, eyes, and more eyes. Dylan's eyes at the White Horse. Among the famous and fallen, Dylan ranks right up there. Some heroes must die badly. As Peter says, Dylan blazed the poet-as-rock-star trail in the public imagination. Still, that *Lux Æeterna* in his eyes haunts me. Some gaze, I think, of the Splendid Thing, as he headed back here to the Chelsea, his home away from home, to lose his earthly consciousness *for ever*.

We all shine on, on and on and on, on and on and on. The back cover of Clarke's *Lost Worlds of 2001*, the vintage copy that I brought with me, offers this Madison Avenue hyperbole:

MIND-BLASTING PROBES INTO
DAZZLING ILLUMINATION

Verily. I discern a burned-in after-imago of Dylan Thomas, a presentiating image, in the stillness of light-speed. (There are no moving pictures of him; he remained, amazingly, unfilmed.) I hold him in my mind's eye, at the bar at the Horse, dancing in flames, so many stars and colliding galaxies in the sky. He was messing with his brain, facing the Void, like an infant he was. From nursery to library to the whole world blowing up. Dylan's deal. Who did he lay down his life for?

It's nearly 3 a.m.—I have written all I can in this alcove window. Night thickens. The tides of sirens and horns are at low ebb. Not long now and they will rise again.

Notes

1. (p. 54) Peter Thabit Jones informs me that neither Paul McCartney nor Bob Dylan has visited the Dylan Thomas Centre in Swansea.

2. (p. 56) *The Edge of Love* had a limited release in the US, to mixed reviews, in March 2009.

3. (p. 57) The death mask of Dylan Thomas was created by New York sculptor David Slivka. A friend of Dylan and Caitlin, Slivka was born on the same day as Dylan. The casting at the Centre in Swansea was at one time owned by Richard Burton and Elizabeth Taylor. A third casting is in the collection of the Smithsonian Institute.

4. (p. 61) The manor house dates to 1723, nine years prior to the birth of George Washington.

5. (p. 78) Later, I wondered if the doll's house was the very one Dylan himself heaved to the front door of the Boat House one Christmas for Aeronwy, as recounted in her book, *A Daughter Remembers Dylan*.

6. (p. 81) Driven to claim the last word, Caitlin published her book, *Leftover Life to Kill*, in 1957.

7. (p. 116) Arthur C. Clarke, *The Lost Worlds of 2001*, page 53. Clarke offers details without diminishing the mystique of creating the "epic drama of adventure and exploration."

8. (p. 116) See http://en.wikipedia.org/wiki/Hotel_Chelsea

9. (p. 117) With Peter Thabit Jones and Stan Barkan, events in New York included Luis Alberto Ambroggio, Mark Barkan, Laura Boss, Sean Bronzell, David Stanford Burr, Neslihan Catto, Sultan Catto, George M. Cook, David Curzon, Aleksey Dayen, Maria Mazziotti Gillan, Leigh Harrison, Robert Harrison, Silvia Kofler, Frank Kunzler, Alyssa A. Lappen, Paul Laursen, Mary Mart, Michael Mart, Beverly Matherne, Ifeanyi A. Menkiti, Liz Metz, Robin Metz, Michela Musolino, Mark Polyakov, Victor Sanchuk, and Bill Wolak.

10. (p. 117) *Dylan Thomas Walking Tour of Greenwich Village, New York*, by Aeronwy Thomas and Peter Thabit Jones, in association with the Welsh Assembly Government in New York, www.dylanthomas.com/index.cfm?articleid=24133

11. (p. 120) Eric W. Sanderson and Markley Boyer, *Mannahatta: A Natural History of New York City*, page 20.

12. (p. 120) See Bob Dylan, *Chronicles, Volume One*. When Bob Dylan arrived in New York from Minnesota, he had already been using his adopted name. He had "seen some poems by Dylan Thomas" and liked the way the name "looked and sounded better" than his given name. The complete story is on pages 78–79.

Resources

Dylan Thomas, *Collected Poems 1934–1952; Collected Stories; Caedmon Collection* [CD box set]

Aeronwy Thomas, *A Daughter Remembers Dylan; Christmas and Other Memories*

John Malcolm Brinnin, *Dylan Thomas In America*

Andrew Lycett, *Dylan Thomas: A New Life*

David Holbrook, *The Code of Night*

Dylan on Dylan, directed by David Sinclair for the Dylan Thomas Estate, documentary feature on *Under Milk Wood* DVD

Dylan Thomas Centre, City and County of Swansea
www.dylanthomas.com

Carmarthenshire County Council
www.dylanthomasBoat House.com

About the Author

John Dotson is an author, artist, and educator who resides in Carmel, California. He was born in 1950 in Kingsport, Tennessee, and is a graduate of Northwestern University. His book *The Enduring Voice* (Mariposa Press, 1987) reflects his experience as the first poet-in-residence of the Robinson Jeffers Tor House Foundation. His poems have been published in the US and internationally and have been translated into several languages. John has written plays that have been produced in the US and in Wales. He has worked in film, video, radio broadcasting, and performance art, and has created a collection of mixed-media sculpture. John taught and was dean of faculty for nineteen years at Santa Catalina School in Monterey. He has taught a wide range of courses in philosophy, psychology, media studies, and creative process at the University of California, Extension, and elsewhere. He is a director of the Monterey Peninsula Friends of C. G. Jung and an active participant in the International Jean Gebser Society for the Study of Culture and Communication.